Healing From The Inside Out

Understanding God's Touch For Spirit Soul and Body

TOM MARSHALL

Sovereign World

Contents

Chapter   Page

    Introduction   5
1. The Basis for Faith   7
2. God's Concern for the Whole Man   17
3. Healing and The Atonement   31
4. Healing and The Kingdom of God   44
5. The Holy Spirit and Healing   54
6. Receiving and Ministering Healing   67
7. Healing and Emotions   83
8. Healing the Human Spirit   102
9. Healing from the Demonic: Deliverance   114
10. The Healing of Relationships   133
11. What happens after Healing?   151

Introduction

Today there is a remarkable and exciting interest in the ministry of healing. We are beginning to understand the amazing dynamic within the Christian gospel to heal all the brokenness of human life. It is beginning to dawn on substantial sections of the church that they are meant to be healing communities; they are not to be mere beneficiaries of the healing ministry, or spectators of the ministry being exercised by a few gifted people, but are intended by God to be active participants.

Once we begin to be open to this dimension of the gospel, however, we face certain problems. Human need is a complex business and we discover that the church is weak on the ground when it comes to foundational resources and 'how-to-do-it' helps. As a result, many Christians are stirred by the possibilities, but lacking properly grounded convictions, give it a go in all honesty and hopefulness. Disappointed by the apparent lack of success, they ruefully conclude that it is not for them.

One of the problems that we face in western society is the existence, even in Christians of some maturity, of a mind that has been programmed by secular humanism, a 'mindset' as Paul calls it in the letter to the Romans. This mindset is anti supernatural, it sees creation as a closed system, it has no place or categories for the intervention (it would say intrusion) of the living God in the world of space and time. That is why we need to have our mind renewed.

The purpose of this book is to provide resources for the re-programming of the mind in terms of the healing ministry, and also a reference point for difficulties that may be experienced along the way. It needs to be used in this way.

It is not a file of healing testimonies. Other books provide that kind of necessary encouragement. It is a means of grounding our faith, not on somebody's experience of healing, or on somebody's healing ministry or reputation, but on the word of God. It should be used as a study book for either individual, group, or seminar use. Read and study it a section at a time. Look up all the scriptures, get hold of the principles, master them in understanding and prove them in experience. I would be thrilled beyond words if I heard of people who took 12 months to work through the book - they would long before that be experiencing the reality of the miraculous.

1
The Basis For Faith

These studies grew out of a double conviction, firstly, that the command to heal the sick and cast out evil spirits cannot be separated from the command to preach the Gospel; secondly, that faith for carrying out of the commands of Christ needs to be firmly grounded on the Word of God. The people who need to have faith for healing are not primarily the sick, but the people who are to heal the sick. Before we can exercise faith, however, we need to know what the Bible teaches. We cannot begin from our own preconceptions about what ought to be the case, or what would be desirable. Faith requires evidence. But the only evidence that God has given to create faith is his Word. We must understand why this is so.

Faith and Knowledge

In spite of what is often taught, Bible faith is never a leap in the dark, nor is it believing without evidence. Biblical faith always rests on knowledge, which is why it always produces results (Hebrews 11:33). Does that surprise you? Perhaps you remember as a non-Christian thinking, ''If only I knew, then I could believe.'' Later, as a Christian, you may have adjusted this view to, ''First you believe, then you know.'' Actually, you were right the first time - you need knowledge or information, and then you have a basis for faith. But the knowledge on which faith operates is knowledge of a particular kind. It is not the kind that reaches us through our senses. It is the knowledge of the will and purposes of God that comes to us by the revelation of the Holy Spirit through the Word of God

"Consequently faith comes from hearing the message and the message is heard through the word of Christ" (Romans 10:17).

In considering the Word of God as the basis for faith we must bear in mind two very important truths. Firstly, God never changes. He says: *"I the Lord do not change"* (Malachi 3:6). *"Jesus Christ is the same yesterday and today and for ever"* (Hebrews 13:8). Secondly, because God never changes, his word never changes *"I will not violate my covenant or alter what my lips have uttered"* (Psalm 89:34). *"Your word, O Lord, is eternal"* (Psalm 119:89).

As far as the subject of healing is concerned, faith needs to know with certainty not only that God is able to heal, but also that he wills to heal. To discover whether this is so, we need to lay aside our presuppositions and allow the Word of God to speak divine knowledge into our heart.

The Origin of Sickness

To understand the nature of healing we first need to understand the nature of sickness; and to understand the nature of sickness, we need to understand the being of man as revealed in scripture.

Man in God's Image

Man made in the image of God occupies a unique place in the order of creation. He is the only created being who inhabits, at one and the same time, both revealed orders of reality: the natural (seen) realm and the spiritual (unseen) realm. Man is, as it were, a bridge between these two realms (2 Corinthians 4:16-18). Note the following points:

1. **Man is a tripartite being: spirit, soul and body** (1 Thessalonians 5:23). From the creation record in Genesis 1:26-27 and 2:7 we learn that:
   a. The human spirit of man was created ex nihilo, out

8

of nothing, and was like God, whose essence is Spirit (John 4:24).

b. The body of man was formed from dust from the ground to which it will return (Genesis 3:19).

c. The soul of man is formed from the relationship between spirit and body (Genesis 2:7).

2. **Man is also a unity,** that is, he functions as one person not as three separate and distinct parts (Deuteronomy 6:5; Psalm 84:2).

a. Because man is spirit, soul and body, but one person, whatever affects one part of his being will affect the other parts also. Thus medical science identifies a wide range of psychosomatic illnesses, where the root causes of disease are emotional rather than physical. The Bible has, however, taught this all along, but has the added insight that both physical and emotional disorders may be spiritual in origin.

"When I kept silent, my bones wasted away through my groaning all day long. For day and night your hand was heavy upon me; my strength was sapped as in the heat of summer" (Psalm 32:3-4).

See also Psalm 31:9-10; 38:3-11; Proverbs 12:4; 18,25; 14:30; 15:30; 16:24; 17:22; 18:21; Mark 2:1-12; James 5:14-16.

What is equally true, but less often recognised, is that it also works the other way around: Physical conditions can affect spiritual and emotional states. Sickness can make us self centred and despairing, or it can cause us to reach out to God (Psalm 102:1-7; 107:17-22; Job 7:5-11; 2 Corinthians 1:8).

3. **Man's life is spiritual in origin.** It was when God breathed the breath (spirit) of life into man's body, that man became a living soul (Genesis 2:7). Without the spirit, the body is dead (James 2:26).

But not only is the spiritual realm the source of man's life, it is also the source of his problems. The tragedy of unbelieving secular man is that because he has a one-dimensional view of two-dimensional reality, he never manages to get to the root of his problems. That is why

9

so many of his best intentioned efforts end up by creating more evils than they solve. Reformatories become schools for crime and welfare systems produce people unable to fend for themselves.

a. **Sin is spiritual in origin.** Sin existed before man was created. It entered into the world by man, as Paul tells us in Romans 5:12, but it preceded him. Sin had its origin in Satan who is a spirit being.

"You were anointed as a guardian cherub,
For so I ordained you
You were on the holy mount of God;
You walked among the fiery stones
You were blameless in your ways
From the day you were created
Till wickedness was found in you
(Ezekiel 28:14-15)

b. **Sickness is essentially spiritual in origin.** It comes from the same source as sin.

"You belong to your father, the devil, and you want to carry out your father's desire. He was a murderer from the beginning..." (John 8:44).

"him who holds the power of death, that is, the devil..." (Hebrews 2:14).

"...he went around doing good and healing all who were under the power of the devil; because God was with him" (Acts 10:38).

The evidence for this origin for sickness is very widespread. It includes express statements as in the book of Job. But also the repeated instances in the New Testament in which sickness is linked directly with the presence of evil spirits - the woman with a form of paralysis caused by a spirit, the epileptic boy and the dumb man who regained his speech when a spirit was cast out (Job 2:-7; Luke 13:11-16; Matthew 9:32-33, 17:14-18).

c. **Demonisation** describes the infestation or oppression of people by evil spirits (Matthew 8:16, 15:22; Mark 1:32, 5:1-15).

Sickness is not always directly linked with demon activity, but it is significant that the healing of sickness and the casting out of demons consistently appear together in the ministry of Jesus and in the life of the early church (Mark 1:32-34; Luke 4:40-41, 13:32; Acts 5:16, 8:7). Jesus' commission to his disciples, which can be summarised as *"Preach the gospel, heal the sick, cast out demons"*, at least suggests a common origin for all three problems: sin, sickness and demon possession (Luke 9:1-2; Matthew 10:7-8).

d.   **Structural evil,** which is the fallenness and rebellion of the institutions of society - the principalities and powers - is also revealed as spiritual in origin (Ephesians 6:12; 1 John 5:19).

The Opening for Sickness

It is clear that neither sin, sickness or death were part of the condition of man as originally created. Man, in other words, was not programmed to die. Death remains an enemy to which he is never reconciled, in spite of centuries of experience to the contrary (1 Corinthinas 15:26.)

In their unfallen state Adam and Eve were immortal, not that they could not die, but there was no need for them to die. Man's mind ruled his body, his spirit ruled his mind and Holy Spirit ruled his spirit. In that state he was a perfect whole being with all his powers, physical, psychological and spiritual in perfect balance, and with no breach through which sin or sickness could come.

The fall brought ruin to man, disrupting not only in his relationship with God, but also his own inner harmony and his relationship with others. Figure 2 illustrates what happened.

1.   Man's human spirit, cut off from God, became open to satanic invasion. (Ephesians 2:1-2; 2 Corinthians 4:4; John 8:44; 1 John 3:10). This opening in man's spirit enables Satan to tempt him to sin, afflict him with sickness and keep him in bondage.

2.   The human spirit lost its power to rule or govern man. Henceforth men are governed by the soul (a domineer-

ing will, a powerful intellect or strong passions) or by the drives and instincts of the body (Philippians 3:19; Proverbs 27:4; 1 Timothy 6:17). The resulting division and disorder in the human personality leads to conditions of stress (Psalm 38:1-18), the predisposing cause of many forms of sickness and infirmity.

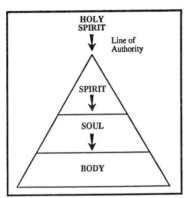 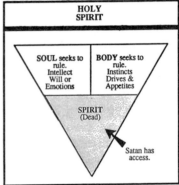

Figure 2

Sickness and Personal Sin

Sometimes sickness is a direct consequence of sin on the part of the sick person. This was the case with the man at the pool of Bethesda to whom Jesus gave the warning: *"Stop sinning or something worse may happen to you"* (John 5:14).

Similarly in the healing of the paralysed man, Jesus linked directly together the forgiving of sins and the healing of the body (Luke 5:18-24). To the church in Corinth Paul writes warning of disorders: *"For anyone who eats and drinks without recognising the body of the Lord eats and drinks judgement on himself. That is why many among you are weak and sick, and a number of you have fallen asleep"* (1 Corinthians 11:29-30).

12

Sickness and Corporate Sin

In spite of the foregoing, there is, in most cases, no direct correspondence between individual sickness and individual sin, although sinful attitudes of bitterness, resentment and unforgiveness may often act as barriers to healing. Nor should we think that every time we, or another person becomes sick, it is because of sin. The disciples of Jesus, apparently subscribing to the sin-sickness doctrine, asked him concerning the man who was born blind, *"Who sinned, this man or his parents?"* Jesus' answer was unequivocal: *"Neither this man nor his parents sinned."* (John 9:2,3).

Our susceptibility to sickness and disease arises mainly because we are part of a sin-affected human race, and live in a world system that is under the rule of the devil (1 John 5:19). In other words, we are as vulnerable to sickness as we are to other human troubles because of our physical, psychological and social solidarity with the rest of the race of men. The link between sin and sickness is generic rather than personal.

It seems clear that the Bible does not promise we will never sin, but it does provide that if we do sin, we have an Advocate, Jesus Christ the righteous one (1 John 2:1). Neither does it say that we, even as christians, will never get sick, but it does provide that if we do get sick there are means for our healing. All the indications in the Bible are that sin and sickness are treated in parallel ways in the economy of salvation.

Does God use Sickness?

It is likely that already the age old question is surfacing in our mind, that is, "Is it always God's will to heal or does God sometimes use sickness?" The answer to the question as to whether God uses sickness is, in my view, clearly Yes. Even although sickness originates with Satan, it is not outside the scope of God's providential dealings with man. In one sense sickness and death are viewed as part of the quarantine that God had to impose on the human race because of sin. God had invested man with such fantastic creative energy and the power to reproduce his kind, that left to himself he could have polluted the universe with his sin and rebellion. Pain, suffering, frustration and death come in with the curse. Man now has to struggle with nature to survive. His life span, hundreds of years before the flood comes down to about 150 and then to 70 years (Psalm 90:10). All the advances of medical science have done little to extend that span.

It took the Cross and the Resurrection to deal with the problem of sin. In the end, therefore, man can come out of quarantine - Christ the first fruits, then those who are Christ's at his coming, and ultimately the whole created order.

Meanwhile it is clear that God uses sickness in a number of ways. Firstly, it is part of the temporal judgement on sin. Our problem is that, even as Christians we do not understand the deadly nature of sin, nor the necessity for God to restrain and check it every time it occurs. Sin left rampant would destroy the universe. Part of the check imposed by God is that when we sin we immediately lose part of our God-given faculties. Always the spiritual senses are blunted and lost, but often sin is allowed to produce its own destructive fruits in man's mind, his body and his relationships.

Secondly sickness is used by God to call men to repentance.

> "Some became fools through their rebellious ways
> and suffered affliction because of their iniquities.
> They loathed all food
> and drew near the gates of death.
> Then they cried to the Lord in their trouble,
> and he saved them from their distress.
> He sent forth his word and healed them;
> He rescued them from the grave. (Psalm 107:17-20)

There are also times when God allows sickness in the lives of his own people. We can identify two main situations: firstly, for the maturing of his saints or for some

14

other higher purpose; secondly, where it is in a sense vicarious, that is, it is for the sake of others rather than the person who is sick. For example, what sort of gospel would we have for people caught in totally meaningless tragedy, if no Christian was ever caught in such a trauma? What gospel would we have for a businessman caught in the undeserved collapse and failure of his life's work, if no christian business ever failed? And what gospel would we have for people in long and painful illnesses, if no Christian ever suffered protracted sicknesses?

Having said all this, there seems to be no biblical warrant for expecting these experiences by God's people to be other than for a limited term, and for a purpose that God can be expected to make abundantly clear to the person concerned.

In spite of the varying interpretations placed upon Paul's thorn in the flesh, it seems more than likely that his suffering was of this nature - a balancing factor left in his life, to protect him from the greater danger of pride over the abundance of the revelation given to him. But Paul was not left to wonder why, he had a clear and satisfying word from God to set his heart at rest. (2 Cor 12:7-9)

Summary

Faith relies on the two facts that God never changes and his word never changes.

To have faith for healing we need to know not only that God is able to heal, but also that he wills to heal.

Man is a unity in which spirit, soul and body are inter-related and interdependent. What happens in his spirit affects his body, and what happens in his body affects his soul and spirit.

Sickness and death are like sin, part of Satan's oppression of the human race so that sickness has a spiritual origin. The healing of sickness, the casting out of demons and the preaching of the Gospel are linked in the ministry of Jesus and the life of the early church.

Man has become subject to sickness and death through sin. Sickness may be a direct cause of individual sin, in which case it disappears when the sin is dealt with. Yet often there is no such direct correspondence. We are vulnerable because of our corporate solidarity with a sin-affected human race and a corrupt world system.

God in his gracious providence nevertheless uses disease, death and other calamities:
- as a temporal judgement against sin,
- to call men to repentance, and
- short term, for higher purposes that he is working out in the lives of his people.

2
God's Concern for the Whole Man

To say that man is a person means that he is an indivisible unity, not a collection of separate parts. Certainly he is spirit, soul and body; but these are never to be considered in isolation. They are interrelated and interdependent: each affects and is affected by the others. Thus the state of my mind can affect my body, or the state of my body can affect my spirit. What happens in my spirit can affect both mind and body.

Man is a spiritual being, but the Bible always treats him as an incarnate spirit. This link between the spiritual and material realms is one of the things that constitutes man's unique significance. So important does it seem to be to the purposes of God, that when man sinned, God did something for him that he did not do for the angels who sinned; he became part of the human race himself, in order to redeem it.

> *"Since the children have flesh and blood, he too shared in their humanity so that by his death he might destroy him who holds the power of death - that is the devil - and free those who all their lives were held in slavery by their fear of death. For surely it is not angels he helps, but Abraham's descendants"* (Hebrews 2:14-16).

The fall affected man's total being. Sin and disobedience alienated him from God and dislocated his whole nature. It brought spiritual, emotional and physical consequences both on the individual and on society. All of these consequences, not merely the spiritual ones, sum up the fundamental state and destiny of fallen man.

17

"For the wages of sin is death" (Romans 6:23).

In salvation God also deals with man as a whole. God has never been concerned merely to save man's "soul", as though the rest was unimportant, or evil, or beneath his notice. When we understand this, we see why the Bible seems to make a clear distinction between those troubles that are external to man's person, and those that invade his person. For example, Jesus never promised that we would escape hardship or persecution or tribulation. In fact the reverse. He said *"in this world you will have trouble"* (John 16:33), but whenever the work of Satan touched the person of man, whether in the form of sin or sickness or demonisation, Jesus always acted to set men free.

The Bible View of the Body

Against the widely held assumption in the church that God is not really very concerned with our physical welfare, we need to see the very exalted view that the Bible has of the human body. Consider carefully the implications of the following.

Firstly, not only man's spirit but his body are shown to be God's handiwork (Genesis 2:7, Psalm 139:13-16). Therefore, on the body was also passed the divine judgement:

> *"Very good."*
> *"God saw all that he had made, and it was very good"*
> (Genesis 1:31)
> *"God gazed on all that he had made, and it was very beautiful"* (Genesis 1:31 - Fenton).

Man's original inheritance was thus not only innocence but health, that is, wholeness in the fullest meaning of the term.

Secondly, in the Incarnation, the Son of God took upon himself a total humanity that included a body created in the virgin Mary's womb. Because Jesus Christ is God in person, we can also say that God has sanctified the human body by experiencing himself all its life, hunger, thirst, weariness, pain, joy and affections. Therefore when Christ came into the world he said *"Sacrifice and offering you did not desire, but a body you prepared for me* (Hebrews 10:5).

Furthermore, the Bible emphasises the essential role of the body of Christ in the work of salvation:

> *"He himself bore our sins in his body on the tree..."*
> (1 Peter 2:24).
> *"This is my body, which is for you..."*
> (1 Corinthians 11:24).

Thirdly, when we come to the new creation in Christ, we find that the whole man, spirit, soul and body is the object of sanctification.

> *"May God himself, the God of peace, sanctify you through and through.*
> *May your whole spirit, soul and body be kept blameless at the coming of our Lord Jesus Christ"*
> (1 Thessalonians 5:23)

Finally, man's ultimate destiny is linked with the resurrection of the body. (1 Corinthians 15:35-42; 1 John 3:2). He is never to be "un-bodied" (2 Corinthians 5:1-4). In fact, the final completion of redemption is described as: *"Our adoption as sons, the redemption of our bodies"* (Romans 8:23).

All this serves to explain the particular attitude that the Bible takes towards sin and sickness as distinct from all other forms of trouble affecting the human race. It explains also why the terms for salvation, health, wholeness, and life are often used interchangeably.

Thus we find that:

1. Salvation and healing are virtually interchangeable terms. The words "cure" and "heal" are used concerning salvation, exorcism and deliverance from evil (Jeremiah 3:22; Hosea 5:13; Matthew 13:15; Acts 10:38). The word "save" is also used of healing (Mark 5:23; Luke 7:50; Acts 4:9-12 etc.)
2. The words whole, wholesome, sound, healthy, besides being applied to physical health and healing (John 5:6,9,11), are used of speech or the tongue (Titus

2:8), of doctrine or faith (1 Timothy 1:10), and also of the heart in the psychological sense (Proverbs 14:30; Psalm 119:80).

What we have presented in Scripture is not salvation for the soul and healing for the body, but a restoration for the whole person that includes his spirit, his attitudes, his body, his imagination, his intellect, his will, his relationships and his societal structures. Salvation is God restoring human life and society to normality, which is *"we will in all things grow up into him who is the Head, that is Christ"* (Ephesians 4:15). and -

> *"be conformed to the likeness of his Son, that he might be the firstborn among many brothers"*
> (Romans 8:29).

Healing and the Covenants

A clear understanding of God's will regarding health and healing is basic to faith. We cannot believe that God will heal unless we know his will on the subject. To discover God's will, we need to turn to the covenants that God has made with man, because this is the form in which God has made his purposes and intentions known. They state what God wills to do for man purely out of his grace. It is not that man has earned or deserves anything from God, but that God has freely chosen so to act towards him.

Covenants also express God's commitment to his promises. In ancient times the covenant was the most solemn and binding of all legal relationships. It was always sealed in blood. It committed the parties to the covenant undertakings in an irrevocable way, and put them under a curse if they ever broke its terms (Genesis 15:8-18; Deuteronomy 29:18-29).

But a covenant is also conditional. God's covenants with man have obligations that man is required to fulfil, in order to participate in the covenant blessings. If he fails to meet these obligations, he forfeits his covenant rights. If he meets these covenant conditions, God has put himself under oath and obligation to make good his promises.

> "I will not violate my covenant or alter what my lips have uttered (Psalm 89:34).
> "Because God wanted to make the unchanging nature of his purpose very clear to the heirs of what was promised, he confirmed it with an oath. God did this so that, by two unchangeable things in which it is impossible for God to lie, we who have fled to take hold of the hope offered to us may be greatly encouraged" (Hebrews 6:17-18).

The covenants of the Old and New Testaments, which are declarations to God's will and purpose, are precise and definite undertakings that God holds out to anyone who will fulfil the covenant conditions. They are written in plain and simple words that anyone can understand, and they declare in straightforward and unmistakeable terms what the will of God is. Let us see the significance of the covenants as they concern healing.

The Old Covenant

The covenant with Israel contained a variety of promises, amongst which a number had particular reference to physical needs.

1. If Israel would be faithful to the covenant, God promised to remove all sickness from their midst (Deuteronomy 7:15). When he brought them out of Egypt there was not one feeble one among them (Psalm 105:37).
2. The covenant blessing of health covered them from birth (no miscarrying or barrenness) to old age, (no premature death) (Exodus 23:26). God's people were promised healing, health and length of days if they walked with him, but sickness, pestilence and death if they did not.
3. The covenant protected the people from epidemics. "Surely he will save you from the fowler's snare and from the deadly pestilence" (Psalm 91:3).

21

4. One of the covenant names of God was Yahweh-rapha *"The Lord the Healing One"*. God's names express his nature or his identity.

    "If you listen carefully to the voice of the Lord your God and do what is right in his eyes, if you pay attention to his commands and keep all his decrees, I will not bring on you any of the diseases I brought on the Egyptians, for I am the Lord who heals you" (Exodus 15:26).

5. The law of God, by which his people were to live, would not be only wisdom to them, but also the source of health for mind and body.

    "My son, pay attention to what I say; listen closely to my words. Do not let them out of your sight, keep them within your heart; for they are life to those who find them and health to a man's whole body" (Proverbs 4:20-22).

Although Israel failed repeatedly and broke the covenant, thus reaping the consequences, instances abound where God still intervened to heal; for example, Miriam in Numbers Chapter 12, King Hezekiah in 2 Kings Chapter 20, and the Shunammite's son in 2 Kings Chapter 4.

The main means by which the covenant promises were acted upon, seems to have been repentance and prayer, often accompanied by sacrifices (Psalm 6:2-9; 2 Kings 20:2-3).

The case of Asa in 2 Chronicles 16:12 is interesting. It is recorded as a failure on his part that when he was sick of a serious disease, *"even in his illness he did not seek help from the Lord, but only from the physicians"*.

The question remains as to what extent the Old Testament promises can be used by Christians today. To get clarity we need to know the essential characteristics of the covenant.

1. Covenants are by their nature everlasting. They represent a bond of personal loyalty between two parties - a superior and a subordinate.

2. Where a subordinate was disobedient he forfeited his

covenant blessings. Nevertheless, the covenant still ran, and the descendants of the subordinate who fulfilled the covenant obligations, automatically fell heir to the covenanted blessings.

"He redeemed us in order that the blessing given to Abraham might come to the Gentiles through Christ Jesus (Galatians 3:14).

3. Because we live under a new covenant today, the safe principle of interpretation appears to be that when an old covenant promise is repeated in a new covenant, it is the will and purpose of God that it be ours today. We will see to what extent this applies to the old covenant promises of healing.

Prophecies about the New Covenant

In the wake of Israel's failure to keep the covenant, we find the prophets beginning to speak of a coming New Covenant that God would offer out of his redeeming grace. This new covenant was sealed in the blood of Jesus Christ, God's Son, so that in the institution of the Lord's Supper he said, *"This cup is the new covenant in my blood."* Many Christians receive the symbol of the New Covenant but do not know what God has promised under the New Covenant.

For example, under the New Covenant, sin, instead of being covered, would be put away. The law of God, instead of being external and written on tablets of stone, would be written on the heart. The Spirit of God, instead of coming only on special men like the prophets, would bring the knowledge of God to all men, from the least to the greatest, and the same Spirit would be poured out in demonstrations of divine power on all flesh. (See Jeremiah 31:31-34; Ezekiel 36:22-28; Joel 2:28).

But the promise of healing also figures prominently in the inauguration of the New Covenant. Consider the all embracing implications of the following New Covenant prophecies:

"Then will the eyes of the blind be opened,
and the ears of the deaf unstopped.
Then will the lame leap like a deer,
and the tongue of the dumb shout for joy"
(Isaiah 35:5-6).

"But for you who revere my name, the sun of right-
eousness will rise with healing in its wings"
(Malachi 4:2).

"I will keep you and will make you to be a covenant for
the people and a light for the Gentiles,
to open eyes that ar eblind,
to free captives from prison
and to release from the dungeon
those who sit in darkness" (Isaiah 42:6-7).

"The Spirit of the Sovereign Lord is on me,
because the Lord has anointed me
to preach good news to the poor.
He has sent me to bind up the broken hearted.
to proclaim freedom for the captives
and release for the prisoners"
(Isaiah 61:1; Luke 4:18-19).

In Hebrews 8:6 we are told that Jesus is the Mediator of a covenant which is superior to the old one and founded upon better promises. If healing is included in the promises of the Old Covenant, how much more is it a part of the better promises of the New Covenant.

The Healing Ministry of Jesus

Christ's ministry abounded in healings. About a quarter of the Gospels are concerned with this side of his ministry, recording about 26 individual healing miracles and some 14 instances of healings of large numbers of people. These are apart from the delegated power to heal that was exercised under Christ's authority by the twelve and the seventy disciples. Nearly twenty percent of the Gospel record is devoted to the healing ministry, far more than that devoted to any other topic or experience.

All who had need of healing and came to him were healed. He made no distinctions, he turned none away, he found no case beyond his power.

We will have cause to return again and again to the healing records in the Gospels, because it is becoming clear that out of all the signs and wonders of Jesus' ministry, the Holy Spirit has recorded these specially selected instances. Properly understood they will cover all the main situations that we are likely to meet today.

When we examine the basis for the healing ministry of Jesus we find the following factors clearly established.

1. Healing of the sick was the fulfilment of the prophecies regarding the New Covenant. For example, healing and the casting out of demons are declared in Matthew 8:16-17 to be the fulfilment of the Messianic prophecy of Isaiah 53:4.

2. When the disciples of John brought the Baptist's question as to whether Jesus was the Messiah, Jesus directed them to his healing ministry as the evidence (Luke 7:21-22).

3. We repeatedly find Jesus addressed by the covenant title, Son of David, in connection with healing, as in Matthew 15:22-28, where healing is also referred to as a covenant blessing, *"the children's bread"*. Note also verse 31 where healing was recognised as the work of the God of Israel, the Covenant God.

4. Healing was unequivocally declared by Jesus to be the will of God. In fact, the source of all Jesus' works was the revelation he received about the Father's works (John 5:19-20).

   In other instances, healing is specifically declared to be the work of God, and evidence of Jesus' union with the Father, for example in the case of the man born blind (John 9:1-5).

All this is summed up in Acts 10:38, in which the healing ministry of Jesus is declared to have its source in the fact that God anointed him with the Holy Spirit. *"How God anointed Jesus of Nazareth with the Holy Spirit and power, and*

*how he went around doing good and healing all who were under
the power of the devil, because God was with him"* (Acts 10:38).

The Church and the Healing Ministry

Because healing is so clearly the will of God, Jesus left his
disciples in no doubt that they were to continue the same
ministry.

1. When after the resurrection, he appeared to them on
    the mountain in Galilee, he commanded them to **make
    disciples of all the nations,** *"teaching them to obey
    everything I have commanded you"* (Matthew 28:20).
    Included in those commandments is Matthew 10:8,
    *"Heal the sick, raise the dead, cleanse those who have
    leprosy, drive out demons."*
    If we make disciples without including these
    commandments, we cannot claim to be fulfilling the
    commission of the Lord of the Church.
2. Jesus also promised that those who believed on him
    would do the works that he has done.
    *"I tell you the truth, anyone who has faith in me will do
    what I have been doing. He will do even greater things than
    these, because I am going to the Father"* (John 14;12).
    The *"greater works"* must refer to those that are
    quantitatively greater rather than qualitatively greater.
    It is hard, for example, to imagine anything greater
    than the raising to life of a man four days dead.
3. The fulfilment of this promise began with the out-
    pouring of the Holy Spirit on the day of Pentecost.
    Immediately we see the same manifestations as in the
    life and ministry of Jesus. The sick are healed, the dead
    raised, demons are cast out and the Gospel is preached
    (Acts 2:43, 3:11, 5:12-16, 6:8, 8:5-8, 9:10-19). The
    church clearly understood this as an essential part of
    their function and as evidence authenticating the word
    of God.

"Now, Lord, consider their threats and enable your servants to speak your word with great boldness. Stretch out your hand to heal and perform miraculous signs and wonders through the name of your holy servant Jesus" (Acts 4:29-30).

4. Nor was this a temporary manifestation confined to the days immediately after Pentecost. Healing marked the entire ministry of the apostles (Acts 14:3, 8:18, 16:16-18, 19:11-12, 20:9-12, 28:3,6-9). Years after Pentecost, Paul writing to the church at Rome, describes what it meant to fully preach the Gospel of Christ.

    "In mighty signs and wonders, by the power of the Spirit of God;
    So that ... I have fully preached the gospel of Christ" (Romans 15:19 NKJV).

    Writing to the church at Corinth, to whom the supernatural dimensions of the life in the Holy Spirit were well-known, he also claims:

    "And my message and my preaching were not with wise and persuasive words, but with a demonstration of the Spirit's power, so that your faith might not rest on men's wisdom, but on God's power."
    (1 Corinthians 2:4-5).

5. The implications of all this for the continuance of the healing ministry in the church today are clear.
    a. If Jesus Christ is the same yesterday, today and forever, then his works are the same, yesterday, today and forever.
    b. If the church is the Body of Christ, then the ministry of the Body must be a continuation of the ministry of Christ. That ministry includes healing.
    c. This was clearly the case in the early church, and there is no scriptural warrant for expecting an era in church life where conditions were to change, so that this model would no longer be so.
    d. The general expectation of the New Testament is that God through Christ will work in people's bodies as well as in their spirits.

Functioning of the Healing Ministry

The availability of healing for the whole person is mediated in a number of ways.

Firstly, any believer who is sick is invited to call for the elders of the church, to pray for him. There is provision for confession, for anointing with oil in the name of the Lord and for the prayer of faith. This repeats similar provisions to those in the old covenant and thus includes healing as a covenant mercy under the new covenant (James 5:14-16).

Secondly, there is the new dimension provided by the power of the Holy Spirit being present to heal, in and through the body of Christ, in the same way as in the ministry of Jesus himself. Thus, the Body is energised and gifted by the Holy Spirit to continue the healing ministry of Christ.

"to another faith by the same Spirit, to another gifts of healing by that one Spirit" (1 Corinthians 12:9).

"And in the church God has appointed first of all apostles, second prophets, third teachers then workers of miracles, also those having gifts of healing..." (1 Corinthians 12:28)

Finally there is provision if neither elders nor healing gifts are available, for healing to be manifested to and through all who believe:

"And these signs will accompany those who believe: in my name ... they will place their hands on sick people and they will get well' (Mark 16:17-18).

Summary

God has always been concerned with the whole man, therefore the Bible presents a very exalted view of the human body. The body is part of God's good creation. In the incarnation his body was integral to our salvation. In the new creation our bodies are the temples of the Holy Spirit, and their members are members of Christ. Salvation is finally the redemption and glorification of the body.

The Bible does not present salvation for the soul and healing for the body, but salvation-wholeness for the whole man - salvation that is healing and healing that saves man at every level of his being.

The covenants express God's will, purpose and disposition towards man. They bind him to make good his promises to those who fulfil the covenant obligations.

The Old Covenant contained clear promises of health, healing and length of days, to those who walked with God. One of God's covenant names, expressing his character, was *"the Lord who heals"*. Even when Israel failed to keep the covenant, and reaped the consequences, God still intervened to heal.

Old Covenant promises remain valid for us today if they are repeated or reaffirmed in the New Covenant.

Prophecies regarding the New Covenant and the Messiah contain many references to healing, and in the ministry of Jesus healing is both the fulfilment of prophecy and evidence of his Messianic office. Healing is expressly declared to be the Father's work, given to Jesus to accomplish, and only possible because God was with him.

It figured prominently in the command given by Christ to his church to preach the gospel, heal the sick and cast out demons.

These manifestations immediately accompanied the outpouring of the Holy Spirit at Pentecost and remained an integral part of the experience and expectation of the early church.

The teaching of the epistles to the church in every age is consistent with this attitude to healing. Not only is every believer invited to seek the Lord for healing as part of the covenanted mercies of the new covenant, but a new dimension is added: the Body of Christ, energised and gifted by the Holy Spirit, continues the healing ministry of Jesus today.

3
Healing and the Atonement

We have seen that both sin and sickness are primarily spiritual in origin. This necessitates that the remedies, forgiveness for the one and healing for the other, must also be sought primarily in the spiritual dimension. Otherwise we are unable to get to the roots of the problems and we deal only with the symptoms. Significantly, forgiveness and healing are always closely linked in Scripture.

"He forgives all my sins and heals all my diseases."
(Psalm 103:3)

"But so that you may know that the Son of Man has authority on earth to forgive sins" ... *then he said to the paralytic. "Get up, take your mat and go home".*
And the man got up and went home."
(Matthew 9:6-7. See also 2 Chronicles 7:14; James 5:15; Matthew 11:5.)

The terms used in the Bible to express salvation and healing are virtually interchangeable - and with very good reason. In human experience it is often not possible to distinguish clearly between what is sin and what is sickness. Sometimes the sicknesses for which we seek healing are, in reality, sins for which we need to repent and seek forgiveness. At other times the sins over which we weep and seek deliverance are really due to sickness or hurt from which we need to be healed. Often they compound one another. Sin cuts off from the life of God and makes us liable to sickness. Sickness makes us anxious and negative and makes it difficult to exercise faith towards God for healing.

To find the way out of this impasse, we need to see not only that sin brought ruin to the whole of man's being, but also that salvation, in turn, deals successfully with all the consequences of sin.

The Complete Fall

Genesis makes it clear that the temptation in the Garden of Eden was not the result of a mere casual encounter, nor was it the exploitation by Satan of a chance opening. It was a skilfully designed and brilliantly executed assault on a broad front that overwhelmed and demolished Eve's defences.

> *"When the woman saw that the fruit of the tree was good for food and pleasing to the eye, and also desirable for gaining wisdom, she took some and ate it. She also gave some to her husband, who was with her, and he ate it."* (Genesis 3:6)

Here is a combined appeal to the whole of Eve's nature. First her senses are enticed and the emotions are stirred. The tree is good for food and a delight to the eyes. Then the mind is captivated by undreamt of possibilities - to be as wise as God, knowing everything. ("The knowledge of good and evil" is a Hebrew idiom for all knowledge.) Finally, the will is ensnared; she takes what is forbidden of God, and relationships are involved. She gives it to her husband and he shares knowingly in the same act. Sin enters human nature.

The effect of sin on man's being was as widespread as his participation in the sin. The whole man reaped the consequences.
1. **Man became mortal,** subject to pain, suffering and death (Genesis 3:16; Romans 5:12).
2. **Struggle and frustration entered into his daily labour.** The ground is cursed and he must toil for his daily bread (Genesis 3:17-19).
3. **Man's powerful emotional responses are perverted.** He is now fearful and repelled by the presence of a loving and gracious God (Genesis 3:10). Moreover he is *"darkened in his understanding"*, so that apart from

the illumination of the Holy Spirit, the ways of God and truth of God are incomprehensible to him (Ephesians 4:18).

4. **The damage extended beyond man's person to his relationships.** Where there had been a loving partnership of equals between the sexes, now there is a desire to manipulate, and the drive to dominate.

"Your desire will be for your husband, and he will rule over you." (Genesis 3:16).

Brotherly love gives way to competition and within a generation, succumbs to hatred and murder.

All these consequences are summed up in the biblical term *"death"* which describes both the present state and the ultimate destiny of sinful man.

"For the wages of sin is death" (Romans 6:23).

The Complete Salvation

The marvel of grace is that when man rebelled against God, and thereby became estranged, it was God who took the initiative to bring man back to himself.

"All this is from God, who reconciled us to himself through Christ and gave us the ministry of reconciliation; that God was reconciling the world to himself in Christ, not counting men's sins against them. And he has committed to us the message of reconciliation."
(2 Corinthians 5:18,19).

There are a number of terms used in the Scriptures to describe the work of God towards man. They all have to do with restoring to an original purpose or design

Redemption   - buying back
Regeneration - bring back to life
Renewal   - making new again
Restoration   - recovering the original plan
Reconciliation - bringing back into harmony

Even salvation has the sense of salvaging something that has been lost or damaged.

Reconciliation

Here we focus on the New Testament theme of reconciliation (Colossians 1:20, Ephesians 2:16; Romans 11:15). We can summarise the thrust of the message as follows.

1. **The meaning of reconciliation.** Reconciliation is to be understood as -
   a. The settling of a difference, dispute or disagreement between two parties.
   b. The bringing back of accord or harmony between the parties by changing their attitudes to one another.
2. **Sin has disrupted man's relationship with God** so that he is now alienated and hostile in mind (Ephesians 2:19; Colossians 1:21), a stranger (Ephesians 2:13), an enemy of God (Romans 5:10), disobedient (Romans 11:30), rebellious (Titus 1:10), and a rejector of God (John 12:48).
3. Reconciliation is the total result of Christ's life and death which permanently changed the relationship between collective man (the world) and God. In other words the aim of reconciliation is to restore man to righteousness (2 Corinthians 5:21).

   When we think of righteousness, we generally have in mind a concept of moral goodness or uprightness,. but this is not primarily the way it is used in the Bible. Righteousness, also translated as being justified, or justification, is used in two main ways.

(a) **It is a relational term.** It means being rightwise or "right with" God, that is, our relationship with him is right; there is no disagreement or difference between us (Philippians 3:8-10)

(b) **It means conforming to the norm or standard.** God is righteous because he is always perfectly what God ought to be. Everything God does conforms perfectly to the absolute standard of his own nature (Psalm 97:2; Romans 1:17).

   This aspect of conformity to the norm is used of man in two very illuminating ways. In Romans 4:3 it says

"Abraham believed God, and it was credited to him as right-eousness." Not only does this mean that faith brought Abraham into a right relationship with God, but also, that in believing God, Abraham conformed to the norm of what man was created to be. Faith, far from being unnatural, is actually the norm or standard for man. He was created to be a God-believing being. Faith, therefore, is in a real sense "natural" to restored humanity.

In Job 33:26 it speaks of God restoring to a man his righteousness. The context in verses 24 to 28 shows that the passage means that God healed him. Health in other words is righteousness or the norm for the body.

4. **If the aim of reconciliation is righteousness, we must also understand that righteousness depends on atonement.** Atonement is the covering of sin by something that makes it lose forever its power to accuse and derange the relationship between God and man. That covering is the Blood of Christ, a term that the New Testament uses to sum up all the results of the death of Christ on the Cross (Ephesians 2:13; Hebrews 9:13-15; Romans 5:9-11).

5. **Atonement requires incarnation.** God gets a footing on both sides of the divide between God and man. The God/Man becomes our mediator (1 Timothy 2:5) and our High Priest (Hebrews 2:17-18).

6. **Atonement necessitates judgement.** God cannot forgive man's sin until man is able to acknowledge God's perfect justice in judging sin and the complete rightness of his wrath against it. Similarly for judgement to be redemptive, its perfect justice must be understood and acknowledged by the one receiving it. Therefore, only a sinless One could be our sin-bearer. Only Jesus, the sinless Man, could perfectly understand and agree with the justice of holiness in its treatment of sin. Therefore at the Cross the holy judgement of God fell on the only place where it could be redemptive.

7. When Jesus died on the Cross he was both
   (a) A Man **for** all men - our **Substitute** (1 Peter 3:18; Isaiah 53:11-12).
   (b) A Man **as** all men - our **Representative** (Hebrews 2:14-18; Galatians 2:20; Ephesians 2:5-6).

Henceforth the Cross has permanently changed the relationship between the world (collective man) and God. Now God can forgive sin, solely on the basis of man's repentance and faith in the redeeming, reconciling work of the Cross.

Is Healing in the Atonement?

The question that concerns us here is this: with which of the widespread consequences of sin does the atonement deal? Does it reach as wide as the damage caused by sin, or does it restore only part of what was lost? Clearly the Cross of Jesus deals with far more than only the guilt arising from sin, fundamental though forgiveness is. All the consequences that followed from the severance of man from the life of God are healed when that relationship is reconciled. **Thus the death and resurrection of Jesus Christ secures for the believer:**

1. **Life in the place of death.** *"The wages of sin is death, but the gift of God is eternal life in Christ Jesus our Lord."* (Romans 6:23).
2. **Forgiveness for guilt.** *"... the Son he loves, in whom we have redemption, the forgiveness of sins."* (Colossians 1:13-14).
3. **Reconciliation for broken relationships.** *"He himself is our peace, who has made the two one and has destroyed the barrier, the dividing wall of hostility ... to create in himself one new man out of the two, thus making peace."* (Ephesians 2:14-16).
4. **Healing for sickness.** *"He himself bore our sins in his body on the tree so that we might die to sins and live for righteousness; by his wounds you have been healed."* (1 Peter 2:24)

Let us look more closely at the specific biblical evidence

that healing is included in the atonement.

1. **There is no doubt that redemption includes the redemption of the body.** *"Not only so, but we ourselves, who have the first fruits of the Spirit, groan inwardly as we wait eagerly for our adoption as sons, the redemption of our bodies."* (Romans 8:23)

2. **Does the awaited redemption also include present healing?** There is abundant evidence that it does.

   (a) Isaiah Chapter 53 is the great Messianic prophecy of the Cross. In verses 3,4 and 10 the words translated "grief" and "sorrow" also means "sickness" and "pain.

"Surely he took up our infirmities" (Choli) (Isaiah 53:4)

"Now Elisha was suffering (Choli) from the illness from which he died" (2 Kings 13:14)

"Even in his illness (Choli) he did not seek help from the Lord, but only from the physicians" (2 Chronicles 16:12)

"And carried our sorrows" (Makob) (Isaiah 15:4)

"A man may be chastened on a bed of pain (Makob) with constant distress (Makob) in his bones" (Job 33:19)

Isaiah 53:10 says that not only was Jesus made guilty with our guilt (the Lord makes his life a guilt offering) but he was also made sick with our sickness (literally means *"He made him sick"*).

We need be in no doubt that this is the correct interpretation of Isaiah 53:4 because in Matthew 8:16-17 we read:

> "... he drove out the spirits with a word and healed all the sick. This was to fulfil what was spoken through the prophet Isaiah: 'He took up our infirmities and carried (margin: 'removed') our diseases.

Moreover 1 Peter 2:24 repeats the message of Isaiah 53:5

> "He himself bore our sins in his body on the tree so that we might die to sins and live for righteousness; by his wounds you have been healed."

The word for "healed" is the Greek **iaomai,** used 26 times in the New Testament, always referring to physical healing. (Matthew 8:8; Mark 5:28).

(b) **In the Incarnation, the Son of God took upon Himself a whole human nature** that he might redeem the whole man. He suffered all the consequences of sin in human nature. He suffered in his spirit and in his mind, in his emotions and in his body. He suffered in the breaking of every human relationship, including his relationship with his Father. Because the fall affected the whole of man's being, it was necessary that redemption restore all that sin destroyed.

(c) In Galatians 3:13 Paul says that Christ *"redeemed us from the curse of the law, by becoming a curse for us."* The curse of the law was the penalty for breaking the law of God. It included sickness, disease and emotional disturbances. (Deuteronomy 28:27-28,35,60-61,65). Therefore Paul says, Christ redeemed us from physical and mental sickness and emotional ills.

(d) Many Old Testament types of the atonement employ images **of physical healing.** For example, we have the cleansing of the leper, Leviticus Chapter 14 (note "atonement" in v.19); the brazen serpent in Numbers Chapter 21, (see John

3:14-15); and in Ezekiel Chapter 47, the tree of Life, whose fruit is for food and leaves for healing.

It is difficult to believe that the fulfilment of the type should provide less than the type itself. If the Cross of Christ brings us far more than the brass serpent brought the Israelites in the wilderness, as it does, it certainly cannot bring us less.

(e) It is in harmony with all the above, that in the New Testament the word "sozo" is used both for "to save" and "to restore or make well."

For the Son of Man came to seek and save (Sozo) what was lost"
(Luke 19:10)

"The prayer offered in faith will make the sick person well" (Sozo)
(James 5:15)

"If you confess with your mouth Jesus is Lord" and believe in your heart that God raised from the dead, you will be saved" (Sozo)
(Romans 10:9)

"Jesus said to him, "receive your sight; your faith has healed (Sozo) you"
(Luke 18:42)

The Significance of Healing in the Atonement

The fact that the atonement deals not only with sin but with sickness has important consequences both for the Church and for individual believers.

1. **Because healing is provided in the atonement the healing ministry of Jesus must continue today.**

If the forgiveness of sins is not confined to the earthly ministry of Jesus, neither can healing be confined to the time of his earthly ministry. Jesus affirmed that this would indeed be so.

"Anyone who has faith in me will do what I have been doing. He will do even greater things than these, because I am going to the Father." (John 14:12)

39

2. It is no surprise therefore that **the Church, after the day of Pentecost, experienced a repetition of the same power manifestations that accompanied the earthly ministry of Jesus.** The dead were raised (Acts 9:36-43, 20:9-12), the sick healed (Acts 5:12-16, 6:8) and demons were cast out (Acts 8:5-8, 16:16-18). The Church's expectation, continually fulfilled, was that the power of the Lord would be manifested to confirm the preaching of the Word.

   "Then the disciples went out and preached everywhere, and the Lord worked with them, and confirmed his word by the signs that accompanied it." (Mark 16:20).

3. **There is no indication in the New Testament that the power experienced by the early Church would ever be withdrawn, or would at some later period be confined to a spiritual or ethical transformation.** The ministry of Jesus through the Church remains the same. His command is to make disciples of all the nations, teaching them to obey everything that he commanded. Jesus' commands can be summarised as - preach the gospel, heal the sick, cast out devils. It is for this that we have been given authority to act in his name (Luke 10:19).

4. **Healing has an important and continuing place in present day evangelism,** because faith is never meant to rest on the persuasive power of argument or reasoning, but on the demonstration of the power of God. That is the clear teaching of the Apostle Paul.

   "My message and my preaching were not with wise and persuasive words, but with a demonstration of the Spirit's power, so that your faith might not rest on men's wisdom, but on God's power. (1 Corinthians 2:4-5).

   (a) Healing and deliverance should be expected as the Gospel is preached and Jesus is proclaimed as the Saviour of the whole person. (Luke 5:31-32).

   (b) In accordance with the experience of the early Church, we can also expect the sick to be healed as a confirmation of the truth of the Gospel, and for God to heal sovereignly as the Word is preached. (Acts 2:41-43; Mark 16:20).

(c) Those who believe in Christ as Lord and Saviour should be prayed for and healed as part of their receiving the benefits of salvation. Some will in fact, first touch Jesus at the point of their need for physical healing. They must of course go on to receive Christ himself; Life which includes salvation and healing is all in him. They are essentially all one provision; he cannot deal with our sicknesses unless we also let him deal with our sin.

But we do not have to improve ourselves, better ourselves or change ourselves first. We simply have to turn from our sin, confess our need, and commit ourselves fully to Christ as Saviour, Healer and Lord. Because he will accept us on these terms, we in turn can accept him and all that comes with him; forgiveness, deliverance, healing, and restoration to wholeness for the whole man.

Healing and the Christian

1. As Christians, we need to realise that redemption is not only **from** sin and its consequences. It is also redemption **back to** God's original purpose for humanity. That purpose is that we might be conformed to the image of Christ, or as Paul expresses it in Ephesians 4:15, *"that we will in all things grow up into him who is the head, that is Christ."* Christ therefore bore all the consequences of man's sin so that he could restore all that man had lost through sin.

2. Just as God made Christ sin for us, so that we need never fear that any **sin** of ours is outside the scope of the atonement, he also made Jesus sick with our sicknesses (the literal meaning of Isaiah 53:10) in order that we need never fear that any particular **sickness** is outside the provision of the atonement.

3. We have seen that although sin is the pre-disposing cause of sickness, it is not necessarily the personal sin

41

of the sick person, but the corporate consequences of the sin of humanity as a whole. Isaiah 53:6 says that *"The Lord has laid on him* (Christ) *the iniquity of us all"*. In other words, the atonement is a corporate provision, although it has to be personally appropriated. It deals with sin not only in terms of guilt, but also in terms of consequences. This means, for example, that there is healing provided from sickness and disease to which we have fallen victim through no fault of our own.

4. There is also deliverance, through the Cross, **from inherited characteristics and traits that may lead us into sin or cause sickness:** for example, a quick temper, proneness to anxiety or congenital weaknesses of body, mind or temperament (2 Corinthians 5:17-18).

Summary

The fall of man involved his senses, emotions, mind and will. Sin therefore damaged every part of man - spirit, soul, body and relationships.

To restore man to righteousness (both a right relationship with God and back to the norm of true humanity), Jesus died as our Substitute and our Representative. He assumed the whole man, to redeem the whole man, and bore all the consequences of sin for the human race, that he might restore all that sin had destroyed. His death and resurrection secures for the believer:

life for death; forgiveness for guilt; healing for sickness, and reconciliation for broken relationships.

Evidence for healing in the atonement includes the following:

* Redemption includes redemption of the body.
* In Isaiah Chapter 53 Christ bore our sickness and pain as well as our grief and sorrow. This is confirmed in Matthew 8:17.
* Christ redeemed us from the curse of the law. The curse included sickness, mental disorder and emotional disturbances.
* Old Testament types of healing include many based on physical healing. The fulfilment cannot be less than the type.
* In the New Testament, "sozo" (save) is also translated "to restore or make well".

Healing, in the atonement, necessitates the continuance of the healing ministry of Jesus. Jesus affirmed this and the early Church experienced and constantly expected it.

For the Christian, it is the assurance that just as no sins are outside the scope of the Cross, neither are any sicknesses. It also provides deliverance from inherited weaknesses, and healing from sickness, to which we have fallen victim through no fault of our own.

Finally, the experience of Salvation-wholeness is dependent on our individual appropriation by faith of Jesus as Saviour, Healer and Lord.

4
Healing and the Kingdom of God

One reason for the virtual disappearance of the healing ministry from the church in past generations, has been its loss (or abandonment) of the central truth of the Kingdom of God. It is not surprising that the recovery of the healing ministry and the renewed emphasis of the Gospel of the Kingdom go hand in hand. They have always belonged together. Healing, it is true, is only part of the Kingdom, but is dependent on the Kingdom, and to the extent that we understand the supreme significance of the Kingdom message, we will again see the Gospel functioning in the demonstration of the Spirit and of power.

What is the Kingdom?

In the Bible, the word "kingdom" does not refer primarily to a place or region, for example the United Kingdom, but to the sovereignty, or right to rule, belonging to a king. For example, in the parable of the talents in Luke Chapter 19, we read that a nobleman went into a distant country *"to receive a kingdom for himself"*. The realm he was to rule was not actually in the far country. He went to his overlord there to receive sovereignty over the place where he already lived.

The Kingdom of God therefore refers to God's sovereignty or government or rule. In this sense there is nothing outside the Kingdom. God's government is universal both in space and time.

*"The Lord has established his throne in heaven,
and his kingdom rules over all"* (Psalm 103:19).

*"Yours, O Lord, is the greatness and the power and
the glory and the majesty and the splendour
for everything in heaven and earth is yours.
Yours, O Lord, is the Kingdom; you are
exalted as head over all"* (1 Chronicles 29:11).

Christ the King

In the Kingdom of God, it is the Father's will that Christ the Son should reign as king. In the New Testament epistles, kingdom truth is therefore characteristically expressed in terms of the Lordship of Christ. Christ the Lord is Christ the King. In other words the Lordship of Christ is another expression for the rule or Kingdom of God.

*"For to us a child is born, to us a son is given,
and the government will be on his shoulders ...*

*Of the increase of his government and peace
there will be no end:* (Isaiah 9:6-7)

*"But about the Son he says,
'Your throne, O God, will last for ever and ever,
and righteousness will be the sceptre of your kingdom"*
(Hebrews 1:8)

*"Therefore let all Israel be assured of this:
God has made this Jesus, whom you crucified,
both Lord and Christ"* (Acts 2:36).

The Kingdom and the Earth

A kingdom is also rule, exercised in a realm and over a body of subjects who recognise the government of the king. It has always been God's purpose to establish his Kingdom on the earth. Genesis opens with God walking on the earth with man; Revelation ends with God dwelling among men on the renewed earth.

"Now the dwelling of God is with men, and he will live with them.
They will be his people, and God himself will be with them" (Revelation 21:3).

What gives planet earth its strategic significance in the universe is the Kingdom. The struggle between God and Satan for the earth has to do with its Kingdom destiny.

The loss of the earth.

Seen in this light the temptation in the garden of Eden was Satan's strategy to foil the purposes of God. His goal was thus

1. To get man to sin. Man thus loses his dominion mandate over the earth and Satan usurps control (John 14:30; Ephesians 2:2; 1 John 5:19).
2. The human race is polluted, therefore God cannot enter it in the person of his son.
3. God can no longer bring his kingdom to earth without its holiness destroying the creation God loves most of all - man.

Thus in the world today we see another kingdom functioning - the kingdom of darkness, that holds men in sin and the darkness of unbelief. Satan is the ruler of this kingdom, and the whole world is under his tragic sway (Colossians 1:13; 1 John 5:19). Sickness and disease are part of his bondage and the demons who are able to take possession of men are his *"angels"* (Luke 13:16; Acts 10:38).

God's plan to renew the earth.

Satan was defeated by the divine wisdom. God's plans were already laid to recover his earth from the usurper. Salvation history is the outworking of that plan.

1. In spite of man's sin, the woman's seed is preserved as the vehicle through which, in the fulness of time, God would enter the human race (Genesis 3:15; Galatians 4:4).
2. The Old Testament records the Kingdom of God intervening in human history. God's providential rule is

seen acting in the affairs of men, notably in the exodus from Egypt and the events of Israel's national history.

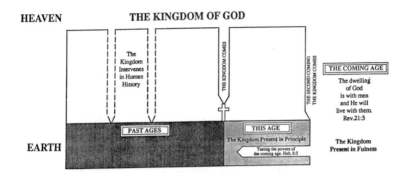

Adapted from the eschatological structure in A Theology of the New Testament by George Eldon Ladd, Lutterworth Press 1975.

3. In the forefront of the prophet's consciousness, there is always the expectancy of a coming of the Kingdom of God, the great and glorious *"day of the Lord"* that will usher in the Messianic age of restoration. Then the great Priest-King (Psalm 110:4; Zechariah 6:12-13), who would be the son of David and yet also the Son of God (Psalm 2:7; 89:27), would rule over an everlasting kingdom. Righteousness and justice would be the foundation of his throne, lovingkindness and truth would go before him. Men would hammer their swords into ploughshares and spears into pruning hooks, and never again would they train for war (Micah 4:3). There would be no more evil or harm and even nature would know release: the wolf and lamb grazing together and lion eating straw like an ox. (Isaiah 65:25).

4. Yet there is a certain ambivalence, because the prophets also saw that same coming of the Kingdom as

a day of gloom and terror, the outpouring of God's wrath in judgement, so that men would hide themselves in the rocks and caves from the great and terrible day of the Lord. The prophets were intuitively aware that, great and glorious as the coming of the Kingdom was, it would be a day of dread for sinners, because the Kingdom would necessarily destroy everything unholy. How, then, can we endure the day of his coming? (Malachi 3:2).

God's problem has never been lack of power to establish his Kingdom on earth. He could do that any time he chose. His problem was to get us into the Kingdom. He had to find a way to deal with our sin so that we could be received into the Kingdom and not destroyed by its coming.

5. There is a further amazing prophetic insight. The King, of the Kingdom, is also the Prophet like Moses; the Suffering Servant of Isaiah Chapter 53; the rejected and smitten Shepherd (Zechariah 11:4-14, 12:10), who will suffer on behalf of men and open in himself, a fountain for their uncleanness (Zechariah 13:1).

The Jews of Jesus' day never managed to put these two figures together. In fact, they generally regarded the King-Messiah, and the Prophet or Suffering Servant as two different persons. The priests and Levites, seeking to identify John the Baptist, asked him, *"Are you the Christ?" "No." "Are you Elijah?" "No." "Are you the Prophet?"* (John 1:19-21). Similarly, the crowds who heard Jesus in the temple at the Feast of Tabernacles were divided. Some said, *"Surely this man is the Prophet."* Others said, *"He is the Christ,"* that is, the Messiah (John 7:40-41).

The Coming of the Kingdom

Suddenly, after 400 years of silence, the public, prophetic voice of God is heard again. From the wilderness, to which Israel always looked for deliverance, comes the voice of one crying, *"Make straight the way for the Lord."* John the

Baptist, the forerunner, comes with his message of the extreme imminence of the Kingdom, *"Repent for the Kingdom of God is at hand."* In fact, the Kingdom is so near that the King, yet unrecognised, is already amongst them.

> *"Among you stands one you do not know. He is the one who comes after me, the thongs of whose sandals I am not worthy to untie"* (John 1:26-27).

The Kingdom of God invades the kingdom of darkness.

The Kingdom comes with the King. The sovereignty and government of God come with the Sovereign.

The presence of the Kingdom was the central theme of Jesus' public ministry from first to last (Mark 1:15; Acts 1:3). It was the recurring motive of most of his parables. *"The kingdom of heaven is like ..."* It was over the question of kingship that he was crucified (Luke 23:1-2, 36-38).

Furthermore in his ministry, Jesus the King of the Kingdom begins to break the tyranny of Satan and begins to dispossess him of his hold over mankind in the following ways.

1. Jesus faces the power of temptation in the wilderness and emerges victorious (Matthew 4:1-11).

2. He heals the sick as a direct attack on Satan's hold over men and women.

   "Then should not this woman, a daughter of Abraham, whom Satan has kept bound for eighteen long years, be set free on the Sabbath day from what bound her?" (Luke 13:16).

3. Jesus casts out evil spirits and declares this to be the coming of the Kingdom.

   "But if I drive out demons by the spirit of God, then the Kingdom of God has come upon you" (Matthew 12:28). Moreover he sends out his disciples, vested with his authority over demons and disease, *"to preach the Kingdom of God and heal the sick"* (Luke 9:1-2).

4. He invades even the realm of death itself, and from the devil, who till then had the power of death (Hebrews 2:14), he takes back the victims - the daughter of Jairus, the widow of Nain's son and Lazarus of Bethany (Matthew 9:24-25; Luke 7:12-15; John 11:43-44).

5. Jesus forgives sin and frees man from the burden of his guilt (Matthew 9:2; John 8:10-11).

6. He reverses the curse on nature and demonstrates man's lost dominion over the earth (Matthew 8:24ff, 14:15ff, John 2:23ff, 21:5ff).

7. He publicly asserts that his ministry is the fulfilment of the prophecies of the Kingdom and nothing less than the inauguration of the Kingdom age, the *"favourable year of the Lord"*

> *"... to proclaim freedom for prisoners and recovery of sight for the blind, to release the oppressed, to proclaim the year of the Lord's favour* (Luke 4:18-19).

8. Finally, on the Cross Jesus dispossesses Satan of his power over man (Hebrews 2:14; John 12:31). By his death and resurrection he destroys every ground Satan has for holding men captive, and disarms the alien powers that rule man's life (Colossians 2:15).

> *"For he has rescued us from the dominion of darkness and brought us into the Kingdom of the Son he loves, in whom we have redemption, the forgiveness of sins"* (Colossians 1:13-14).

9. In the present age the church is the emissary of the Kingdom (Matthew 16:18-19). Jesus' final post-resurrection instruction of the disciples was concerning the Kingdom (Acts 1:3-4). It was with this in mind that they were commanded to wait for the outpouring of the Holy Spirit. It is no surprise, therefore, to find Peter, on the day of Pentecost, identifying that outpouring with Joel's prophecy regarding the coming of the Kingdom - the *"Day of the Lord"* (Joel 2:28; Acts 2:16-21).

The Presence of the Kingdom

Although the Jews of Jesus' day were looking for Messiah as the coming King, they did not recognise him when he came. In his parables Jesus explained the mystery of the Kingdom. The central message includes the following important points.

1. The Kingdom of God is both present and future. It has already come (Matthew 12:28), but we are to pray for its coming (Matthew 6:10).
2. The Kingdom which belongs to the age to come (Matthew 13:39-42), is therefore already present among men in advance, but in an unexpected form (Matthew 13:33).
3. The Kingdom is open now for man to enter, on God's terms; that is, by repentance and a new birth through the Holy Spirit (John 3:3-5). But man can also reject the present Kingdom.
4. Although the Kingdom in its fulness belongs to the age to come, inaugurated by the Second Coming, yet the Kingdom blessings of the age to come can be realised in this present age (Isaiah 32:2-4; Hebrews 6:5).
   a. In the Kingdom to come there will be immortal life; in the Kingdom now there is healing.
   b. In the Kingdom to come the devil's power will be totally destroyed;
      in the Kingdom now we have power to cast out demons.
   c. In the Kingdom to come we will be perfect;
      in the Kingdom now we are sanctified and can know real victory over sin.
5. The church has been commissioned to preach the Gospel of the Kingdom in all the world for a testimony. This is the most important of all end-time signs (Matthew 24:14), and the church's primary responsibility today.

The Gospel of the Kingdom is the Gospel of salvation with the addition of the powers of the age to come. Jesus went through the cities and villages *"teaching in*

51

their synagogues, preaching the good news of the Kingdom and healing every disease and sickness" (Matthew 9:35). Every time we pray, "Your Kingdom come," we are asking for these same evidences of the Kingdom to take place, because the Kingdom is meant to be demonstrable: it is not word but power (1 Corinthians 4:20).

6. The miraculous - works of healing and deliverance - are distinctive Messianic signs, they are evidences of the Kingdom's presence. Although John the Baptist recognised Jesus at the Jordan as the Suffering Servant, the Lamb of God (John 1:29), it seems that he did not realise that he was also the King. Later, he sent his disciples to Jesus to ask him. *"Are you the one who was to come?"* Jesus' response was to heal the sick and to say to the disciples, *"Go back and report to John what you have seen and heard: The blind receive sight, the lame walk, those who have leprosy are cured, the deaf hear, the dead are raised and the good news is preached to the poor"* (Luke 7:22).

7. The Rock on which the church rests, so that the gates of hell will not prevail against it, is the kingship of Christong
    (Matthew 16:15-18), a *"Kingdom that cannot be shaken"* (Hebrews 12:28).

8. The church, as the Messianic community, is to express the power, the character and the values of the Kingdom (Matthew 13:38; Luke 12:31-33). For this purpose it has been given the keys of the Kingdom (Matthew 16:19). The keys of the Kingdom are the keys that lock heaven and earth together in power, in other words the prayer of faith that can:
    a. **Bind** the strong man (Satan) and spoil his goods (Luke 11:21-22).
    b. **Loose** those bound by Satan (Luke 13.16).

9. The power of the Kingdom is spiritual (2 Corinthians 10:3-4), its weapons are spiritual (Ephesians 6:10-18), and they are totally adequate for the destruction of all Satanic powers (1 John 3:8, 4:17).

Summary

The Kingdom of God is God's rule or government, and the Father's will is that Christ be King of the Kingdom.

God's purpose has always been to establish his Kingdom on the earth and to give man a place in it. But man has partaken of Satan's rebellion and is now captive to his power, bound by fear, sin, sickness and the domination of evil spirits.

Because the coming of the Kingdom would destroy all evil, and therefore sinful man also, God had to find a way, not only to bring the Kingdom to earth, but to get man into the Kingdom without being destroyed.

In the Incarnation, the Kingdom of God, in the person of the King, invaded the domain of darkness. Immediately the King begins to expel the usurper. He defeats temptation, heals the sick, casts out evil spirits, raises the dead, reverses the curse on nature and forgives sin. All these are declared to be evidences of the presence of the Kingdom.

Finally, by his death and resurrection, Jesus broke the power of Satan over the human race, and made a way for us to enter the Kingdom through the new birth.

When Christ came, the presence of the Kingdom was not recognised by the Jews because the King was also the Suffering Saviour, and the Kingdom came in an unexpected form. It is present in a form that can be accepted or rejected by men. The Kingdom that belongs to the age to come, will come in fulness at the Second Coming; but it is already realised in principle in the present age. The church as the agent of the Kingdom, has the Gospel of the Kingdom, that is, the Gospel of salvation with the addition of the Kingdom powers of the age to come. The church has authority over the devil's works. It has the keys of the Kingdom that can bind the power of Satan, and loose man from his tyranny of sin and sickness.

Kingdom life and Kingdom authority are based on total obedience to the will of the King and on the revelation of Kingdom life and Kingdom power.

5
The Holy Spirit and Healing

Sickness, like sin, is essentially spiritual in origin. There-fore, from the very beginning, God's method of healing has been spiritual. This can be seen even in healings recorded in the Old Testament, for example the incident of the brazen serpent in the wilderness (Numbers 21:8-9) or the healing of Miriam from leprosy (Numbers 12:10-13).

For both of these spiritual problems, sin and sickness, God has provided the perfect solution by the death of Jesus Christ on the Cross. Through the atonement God can justly forgive all our sins and heal all our diseases. (Psalm 103:3).

Now we have to learn exactly how God applies the work of the Cross to meet our needs. It is important to understand this, so that knowledge can be translated into experience. On the one hand the work of the Cross is objective and external, that is, it is outside us. Christ did it by himself on our behalf. Because God did it completely by himself, we know that it is both a perfect work and an eternal work. On the other hand my needs are subjective and internal; guilt and sickness are within me. How then do I obtain the grace available through the Cross, so that it comes within me to release me from guilt and to heal me from pain and sickness? This is the particular ministry of the Holy Spirit.

The Holy Spirit the Life-Giver

It was always God's plan from the beginning that man should be indwelt by the Holy Spirit. In the Garden of Eden there is not only the Tree of Life that speaks of Christ but there is a river that speaks of the Holy Spirit (Genesis 2:9-10). God always intended to be not only "God with us" but also "God in us". **In the first creation** it was the Holy Spirit who created man's human spirit. As Jesus tells us in John 3:6, spirit is born of Spirit. Furthermore when man's body was formed from virgin soil it was the Holy Spirit who breathed life into it.

> "The Lord God formed man from the dust of the ground and breathed into his nostrils the breath of life, and man became a living being." (Genesis 2:7)

> "The Spirit of God has made me; the breath of the Almighty gives me life." (Job 33:4).

When the first man fell into sin and death, it was the Holy Spirit who again brought Life into the world in the person of the Redeemer, born of a virgin mother.

> "The angel answered, 'The Holy Spirit will come upon you, and the power of the Most High will overshadow you. So the holy one to be born will be called the Son of God'." (Luke 1:35)

In the new creation Christ is the Life (John 1:4,14:6) but the Holy Spirit is the Life-giver who gives that life to redeemed men and women. He is the Spirit of Life who sets us free from the law of sin and death. (Romans 8:2)

> "He has made us competent as ministers of a new covenant - not of the letter but of the Spirit; for the letter kills, but the Spirit gives life." (2 Corinthians 3:6)

The Holy Spirit the Agent of Healing

It is important to understand that in the Incarnation, Jesus lived a fully human life on genuinely human terms. All that he did in his public ministry he did as a man filled with the Holy Spirit.
* He was baptised in the Holy Spirit at the River Jordan (Matthew 3:13-17; John 1:32-33).

* He was led by the Holy Spirit into the wilderness (Luke 4:1; Mark 1:12).
* He returned in the power of the Holy Spirit (Luke 4:14).
* He was anointed with the Holy Spirit to preach (Luke 4:18).
* He healed by the power of the Holy Spirit (Acts 10:38).
* He cast out demons by the power of the Holy Spirit (Matthew 12:28).

Thus even the miracles Jesus performed have a particular characteristic - they are all miracles that a man can do if he is filled with the Holy Spirit. The power displayed by Jesus, though very remarkable, is something less than omnipotent. In his home town, for example, it is said that

"He could not do any miracles there, except lay his hands on a few sick people and heal them. And he was amazed at their lack of faith." (Mark 6:5).

There was another reason for this self-imposed limitation. We find it in John 14:12, *"I tell you the truth, anyone who has faith in me will do what I have been doing. He will do even greater things than these, because I am going to the Father."* In other words **Jesus was modelling a ministry that his disciples would be able to follow.**

* The Holy Spirit was the power (dunamis) of the Lord who was present to heal in Jesus' ministry. (Mark 5:30; Luke 5:17, 6:19, 8:46).
* He was the "finger of God" who expelled demons (Matthew 12:28 cf Luke 11:20).
* The disciples who had lived with Jesus for three years knew the presence and power of the Holy Spirit in his life. In this sense the Holy Spirit had been with them also. (John 14:26)
* They had the promise of Jesus that the same power (dunamis) would be theirs through the same Spirit. (Luke 24:49; Acts 1:8).

The Post Pentecost Experience

We are inclined to think that the day of Pentecost took the

disciples completely by surprise, but that is not the case. Although some of the phenomena may have been unexpected, the general tenor of what Jesus promised was not. They waited and prayed and pondered the prophetic scriptures, so that when the Holy Spirit came, we find the apostles moving immediately and confidently in the new dynamic. (Acts 2:43, 5:12-16, 6:8,9-17, 8:4-8, 9:32-41, 10:1ff etc).

The ministry of Jesus is repeated again and again. The sick are healed, the dead raised, demons are expelled and the Gospel is preached in the demonstration of the Spirit and of power. Thus Paul in writing to the Romans can describe his ministry in the following terms - *"by the power of signs and miracles, through the power of the Spirit ... I have fully proclaimed the gospel of Christ."* (Romans 15:19).

The Gifts of the Holy Spirit and Healing

The place of the Holy Spirit in healing is clearly seen in the gifts of healing and miracles which are said to be "manifestations" of the Holy Spirit.

> *"To each one the manifestation of the Spirit is given for the common good ...*
> *to another gifts of healing by that one Spirit, to another miraculous powers."*

Here we are moving in a different dimension from praying for the sick. By and large, we do not find the apostles preaching healing or praying for the sick. They preached the **Gospel** and **healed** the sick. (Acts 9:17-18, 6:8, 14:8-10)

Healing, as one of the spiritual gifts in 1 Corinthans Chapter 12, is not so much a single gift, but a wide-ranging and varied spectrum of gifts. The term used, "gifts of healing" is at least suggestive that a degree of specialisation may even operate. The exercise of the gift of healing differs from praying for the sick in two main ways.
1.   It is often independent of any requirement of faith on the part of the sick person. The faith - for faith there must be - is possessed by the person through whom

the gift is manifested. For example, there is no evidence of faith for healing by the lame man at the temple gate. There is nothing to suggest that he asked for, or expected, anything but money. The faith in the name of Jesus referred to in Acts 3:16 is the faith of Peter and John. Similar factors occur in the healing of Aeneas in Acts 9:33-34 and the father of Publius:

"His father was sick in bed, suffering from fever and dysentry. Paul went in to see him and, after prayer, placed his hands on him and healed him." (Acts 28:8)

2. The person through whom the healing gift is manifested needs to know the mind of the Lord for the individual and for the occasion. There is often the operation of the word of knowledge, in association with the gift of healing (Acts 9:10-17).

Miracles

Overlapping the gift of healing is the gift of miracles. We must be careful about making any hard and fast categories of the spiritual gifts, but we can perhaps distinguish a miracle from a healing, in that miracles are cases of dramatic and instantaneous healings.

The gift of healing results in the recovery of the sick person - not necessarily immediately, although it may be so. The gift may work in a natural, gradual and progressive manner. The gift of miracles refers to works of supernatural origin and character such as could not possibly be produced by natural agents and means. Thus the healing of the lame man was a "noteworthy miracle". (Acts 4:16). See also Acts 19:11-12.

"God did extraordinary miracles through Paul. Handkerchiefs and aprons that had touched him were taken to the sick, and their illnesses were cured and the evil spirits left them."

From this we see that the gift of miracles is also the means whereby deliverance is ministered to those afflicted by evil spirits.

Finally, a miracle is an attesting sign that is intended to bring a revelation to those who see it, both of the person of Jesus and of the truth of the Gospel. Its purpose, therefore, extends beyond the mercy received by the individual. We can almost say that, while a healing may take place in private, a miracle is always meant to be public or publicly known. (Acts 9:33-42)

Discerning of Spirits

The purpose of the gift of discerning of spirits is to distinguish those cases where the cause of sickness, emotional disturbance or personality disorder, is the presence of evil spirits (Matthew 9:32-33; Mark 9:17-27; Luke 13:10-13). It cannot be over-emphasised that **the presence of evil spirits can be known only by discernment:** It should never be assumed from lists of symptoms or external evidence. In Matthew Chapter 17, the epileptic boy was the victim of a demon, but in Matthew 4:24 demoniacs and epileptics are separate categories, showing that not all epileptics are cases of demonisation. An example of the operation of the gift is also found in Paul's early ministry in Philippi. (Acts 16:16-18)

Receiving Spiritual Gifts

The Bible is quite clear that the spiritual gifts are manifestations of the Holy Spirit, given as he wills and to whom he wills. Furthermore, they are given for the common good, not for personal profit or advancement. (1 Corinthians 12:4-7, 28-30)

Nevertheless, there is a part we have to play in their being manifested in the Church.

1. **We are to seek them.** In fact, we are told to earnestly desire them, especially the greater gifts. (1 Corinthians 12:31, 14:1)
2. **We are to ask for them.** (Matthew 7:7-11, cf Luke 11:9-13)

3. While they are given by the Holy Spirit, the means that He uses to impart them is often **by ministry from others.** Paul longed to impart some spiritual gift, that is, share something that he himself had, or experienced. (Romans 1:11; 1 Timothy 4:14)
4. **Faith is an essential element** both in receiving spiritual gifts and in exercising them. (Acts 6:5,8; Matthew 17:20-21; Galatians 3:5)

Exercising the Gifts of Healing and Miracles

The gifts of the Holy Spirit are given to enable the Church to fulfil the command of Christ, that is, to preach the Gospel, to heal the sick and to cast out demons. But the operation of spiritual gifts also places certain demands on the person through whom they are manifested.
1. **The necessity for compassion,** that is, a heart that is always open towards others (Matthew 20:29-34). This is different from sympathy, which can stir our feelings towards some, and not towards others, to some situations but not to others. Compassion is an openness of heart to all men. (2 Corinthians 6:11)
2. **The ability to discern the presence of the Spirit's power.** It is clear that even in the ministry of Jesus, His experience of the power of the Holy Spirit was not always the same. Instances are recorded when *"the power of the Lord was present for him to heal the sick"* (Luke 5:17).

   "And the people all tried to touch him, because power was coming from him and healing them all." (Luke 6:19)
3. **An attitude of self-giving towards the needy person.**
   "Silver or gold I do not have, but what I have I give you. In the name of Jesus Christ of Nazareth, walk!" (Acts 3:6). It is questionable whether we can give anything of God to another person without also giving ourselves.
4. **Faith,** that is largely independent of the need, or the attitude of the other person (Acts 9:34). But at times, the faith of the sick person is significant. (Acts 14:8-10)

5. **A knowledge of the mind of the Lord for the situation** (Acts 9:40, 20:9-10; Mark 5:35-42).
6. **Periods of prayer (and fasting)** (Mark 9:29 marg; Luke 6:12 cf v 19)

Symbols of the Holy Spirit in Healing

The special ministry of the Holy Spirit, in the realm of healing, is further evidenced by the **symbols** used in the ministry of healing, in particular anointing with oil and the laying on of hands.

We need to understand the biblical usage of symbols. To our modern, Western mind, "symbol" has come to convey the ideas of a substitute, or a mere representation, in place of the real thing. But, in the Bible a symbol is not a substitute for the real thing, it is the means whereby the real thing is communicated or mediated. The Ark of the Covenant was not a substitute for the Presence of God amongst his people; it was the means whereby the Holy Presence was realised (2 Samuel 6:6-7). A kiss is not a substitute for love, but a symbol - a means through which love is conveyed. What shocks us about the kiss of Judas is that he turned the symbol of love into the means of betrayal.

1. **Anointing with oil** (James 5:14; Mark 6:13). The symbol of anointing speaks of the Holy Spirit (Isaiah 61:1,2; 2 Corinthians 1:21-22; 1 John 2:27; Acts 10:38). "Christos" means "His Anointed". In the ministry of healing, anointing with oil, when done in faith and in obedience, becomes the means whereby the Holy Spirit touches, or comes upon, the sick body.
   "Is any one of you sick? He should call the elders of the church to pray over him and anoint him with oil in the name of the Lord. And the prayer offered in faith will make the sick person well; the Lord will raise him up. If he has sinned, he will be forgiven." (James 5:14-15)
2. **Laying on of hands.** One of the Old Testament titles for the Holy Spirit is "the Hand of the Lord". The Hand of the Lord coming on the prophet, and the Spirit of the Lord coming on the prophet are inter-

changeable terms. (Ezekiel 1:3 cf 11:5). The Hand of the Lord is also the power of the Lord (Habbakuk 3:4) so that when in faith we lay hands on the sick, the Spirit of the Lord, who is also the power of the Lord, comes upon them to heal them or set them free.

"When Jesus saw her, he called her forward and said to her, 'Woman, you are set free from your infirmity.' Then he put his hands on her, and immediately she straightened up and praised God." (Luke 13:12-13)

"And these signs will accompany those who believe ... they will place their hands on sick people, and they will get well." (Mark 16:17-18)

How the Holy Spirit Heals

We have seen that sickness and sin are the work of Satan who is a spirit being. The out working of both in man is death. Healing is part of the saving, restoring work of God. Through Christ's death on the Cross the ground for Satan's oppression of the human race is dealt with. Now the Holy Spirit steps into the breach.

Because of the death and resurrection of Jesus, the **Holy Spirit is able to roll back the work of Satan in us.** One day it will be rolled back so far that death itself will be swallowed up by immortal life (1 Corinthians 15:54). Even now death is no longer a terminal experience for the christian; it is a doorway to be with Christ, which is far better. But one day death itself, the last enemy will be destroyed. (1 Corinthians 15:26).

In Romans 8:2 the Holy Spirit is called the "Spirit of Life." The names of the Holy Spirit, like the names of God and the names of Christ, are a revelation of his power and his nature. Because he is the Life-giver, everything he touches must live (Ezekiel 47:1-9). Romans 8 explains this in some detail.

a. The indwelling of the Holy Spirit brings life to the believer's human spirit.

"You, however, are controlled not by the sinful nature but by the Spirit, if the Spirit of God lives in you. And if anyone

does not have the Spirit of Christ, he does not belong to Christ. But if Christ is in you your body is dead because of sin, yet your spirit is alive because of righteousness." (Romans 8:9-10)

b. The presence of the Holy Spirit brings life to the believer's mind.

"The mind controlled by the Spirit is life and peace." (Romans 8:6b)

c. The presence of the Holy Spirit gives life to the believer's body.

"And if the Spirit of him who raised Jesus from the dead is living in you, he who raised Christ from the dead will also give life to your mortal bodies through his Spirit, who lives in you." (Romans 8:11)

The ultimate consummation of this indwelling will be the redemption of the body from death to immortality (Romans 8:23; 1 Corinthians 15:42-44, 52-54).

Faith and Confession

There is something further required before the power of the Holy Spirit can touch the areas of sickness in our body, or disturbance in our mind. A response is necessary on our part. Although the Holy Spirit indwells the believer, he does not take over our personality. He will never intervene in any area of our life unless there is the free response of the human will. There are two dimensions of this response that are of great importance. We discuss them here in terms of healing, but they have a much wider significance.

1. **Faith** is not an arbitrary condition laid down by God as the basis for us to receive his blessing. **Faith is a necessary condition.** It is the free response of our heart to the love of God. Bible faith is much more than mere intellectual assent. It is the whole of our inner nature saying "Yes!" to the inner prompting of the Holy Spirit. The need is that faith be real - not that faith be great. A fuse wire may only be a 5cm length of 10 amp wire, but without it all the current in the system will

not light a single bulb. Put the little fuse wire in place and you can run an entire factory.

When we reach out in faith to the reality of the indwelling Spirit, as the vehicle for the promises of God to be fulfilled, we insert the fuse wire in the power system of the Almighty.

"Go," said Jesus, "your faith has healed you." Immediately he received his sight and followed Jesus along the road." (Mark 10:52)

2. **Confession.** The link between faith and confession is very important. Confession is the consent of the heart and lips to what God says.

"If you confess with your mouth "Jesus is Lord" and believe in your heart that God raised him from the dead you will be saved (sozo). *For it is with your heart that you believe and are justified, and it is with your mouth that you confess and are saved* (soteria)" (Romans 10:9,10). Sozo and soteria mean both saved and healed.

A very important principle is involved in confession.

a. God, the uncreated Creator, creates by his word, that is, by speaking things into existence. God said, *"Let there be light"* and there was light. (Genesis 1:3)

    "By the word of the Lord were the heavens made, their starry host by the breath of his mouth." (Psalm 33:6)
    "By faith we understand that the universe was formed at God's command." (Hebrews 11:3)

b. Man is a created creator. He creates in the same way as God creates, by speaking into existence what is in his heart, whether good or bad.

    "For out of the overflow of the heart the mouth speaks. The good man brings things out of the good stored up in him, and the evil man brings evil things out of the evil stored up in him." (Matthew 12:34-35)

    Often, therefore, what we receive in our faith has to be spoken into existence. This speaking is confession.

"For verily I say unto you, that whosoever shall say unto this mountain, ''Be thou removed, and be thou cast into the sea; and shall not doubt in his heart, but shall believe that these things which he saith shall come to pass; he shall have whatsoever he saith." (Mark 11:23 AV)

"It is written: 'I believed: therefore I have spoken'. With that same spirit of faith we also believe and therefore speak." (2 Corinthians 4:13)

In the public ministry of Jesus we find that he moved constantly in the realm of faith-confession which is why he taught it as a principle. (John 11:23, 41-42; Matthew 15:28 etc.)

"He said 'Go away, the girl is not dead, but asleep,' but they laughed at him." (Matthew 9:24)

Whatever Jesus did when he healed the sick he almost always spoke a word - *"I will, be clean." "According to your faith be it done to you." "Rise, take up your bed and walk."*

c. **Confession follows faith;** it is not a substitute for faith. If there is no faith, all we have is mind over matter, or the power of positive thinking. That can be sheer presumption, but often when we have received something in our faith, it will not come to pass until we speak it in words. (Mark 11:23)

In such ways as these, we need continually to present our bodies as a living sacrifice, so that they may become temples of the Holy Spirit. We must allow the Spirit to deal with wrong attitudes, disobedience, unbelief and sin. We must ask him to fill us with his power and grace and health. If we do, we will find that he will solve our conflicts, cleanse our thoughts, and stimulate right thinking, right feelings and right attitudes. The end result will be not only healing, but health.

Summary

Because sickness is spiritual in origin, God provided in the atonement the spiritual answer to the problem, and in the Holy Spirit has given One who can roll back the death work of Satan in us.

The Holy Spirit is the Life-Giver. In the ministry of Jesus He was the anointing, the power of the Lord, and the finger of God. The early Church received the same power at Pentecost.

Anointing with oil, and the laying on of hands, are symbols of the Holy Spirit, and means by which his presence and power are mediated.

The spiritual gifts, which are manifestations of the Holy Spirit, include several directly related to the ministry of healing - gifts of healings, the gift of miracles and the gift of discerning of spirits.

The gift of healing results in the recovery of the sick person - not necessarily immediately, although it may be so.

The gift of miracles produces dramatic, instantaneous healings of supernatural character such as could not be produced by natural means. Discerning of spirits distinguishes those cases where sickness is due to the presence of evil spirits.

Spiritual gifts are in the sovereign will of God, but we are to seek them earnestly, ask for them, impart them to one another and believe for them. They are given to equip the Church to carry out Christ's command: preach the Gospel, heal the sick, cast out demons.

6
Receiving and Ministering Healing

We have seen that it is God's will to make men whole from all the consequences of sin, including guilt, sickness, and enslavement to habits or evil spirits. In the atonement, Christ provided a basis on which he can forgive all our sins and heal all our sicknesses, and the Holy Spirit is the effective agent who accomplishes these things in us.

Understanding God's provision, however, does not make it ours. There needs to be faith to appropriate it for ourselves, or for others to whom we are called to minister.

The Model for the Ministry of Healing

There is a wealth of teaching and information in the Gospels and the Acts of the Apostles about the healing ministry of Jesus and that of the early church. It is clear that the miracles reported are only a few of many more healings that took place. These particular ones are however very important because they have been selected by the Holy Spirit to be recorded for our benefit.

> *"Jesus did many other miraculous signs in the presence of his disciples, which are not recorded in this book.*
> *But these are written that you may believe that Jesus is the Christ, the Son of God, and that by believing you may have life in his name"*
> (John 20:30-31).

What has never been given sufficient attention, is that

the New Testament miracles, properly understood, cover all the possible circumstances we may find ourselves concerned with in the healing ministry.

The details that are given of the miracles are not just background or local colour; nor are they merely intended to be used to illustrate spiritual truths. They contain the keys to the healing - and the reasons why certain principles were used in the particular instances that are described, because there was no standard or routine way in which Jesus, or the apostles, exercised their healing ministries.

With this in mind, we can now turn to some of the factors which emerge from an analysis of the healing ministry of Jesus, both in his own public ministry and through his church.

The Scope of the Healing Ministry

There are detailed records in the Gospels and Acts of a large number of both individual healings or deliverances, and mass healing and deliverance. The following factors emerge from a study of the data.

1. Healing applied to all manner of complaints including:
   a. Relatively minor illnesses such as fever (Matthew 8:14-15).
   b. Advanced stages of disease such as the man *covered with leprosy* (Luke 5:12).
   b. Chronic states: the woman who had a haemorrhage for 12 years, or the man at the pool of Bethesda who had been sick for 38 years (John 5:1-14; Mark 5:33-4; Acts 9:32-33).
   d. Congenital conditions, that is, people affected from birth - the blind man or the lame man at the temple gate (John 9:1-4; Acts 3:2, 14:8).
   e. Terminal conditions, those at the point of death (John 4:47), including those who had actually died (Luke 8:40-56, 7:11-17; John 11:1-44). The latter seem to have always been those who had died before their due time.

68

f. The results of accidents and assaults (Acts 20:9-10; Luke 22:50-51).
g. Psychosomatic disorders (Matthew 9:2-7).
h. Results of demonic affliction (Matthew 9:32-34, 12:22; Luke 8:27-35).

2. The presence of pain aroused an instant response on the part of Jesus. When the Roman centurion said of his servant, "... (he) *is paralysed and in terrible suffering*", Jesus' immediate response was "*I will go and heal him*" (Matthew 8:5-7).

3. Healings included not only individual healings, but numbers being healed simultaneously, for example, the ten lepers (Luke 17:11-19).

4. Both healing and deliverance took place with the afflicted person present and at a distance, in at least one case over 50 km away (John 4:46-54; Matthew 8:5-13; Mark 5:1-20, 7:24-30).

The Methods used in Healing

When we examine the methods used in ministering healing, we find a similar diversity, the significance of which needs to be pondered.

1. A common method used by Jesus was to touch the sick person. He touched blind eyes (Matthew 9:27-31), put his fingers into deaf ears (Mark 7:32-37), and touched the leper (Matthew 8:3). In even greater identification we find Jesus taking Jairus' daughter by the hand, and Peter seizing the lame man by the hand and raising him up (Matthew 9:25; Acts 3:6-7). Touch is also the point of contact for faith.

2. Closely related to this is the laying on of hands for healing (Mark 6:5; Luke 4:40; Acts 9:12). The special significance of this has already been discussed.

3. Commanding healing or rebuking the sickness (Luke 4:39; Mark 7:34; Acts 14:10). In the great majority of cases, **regardless of what else was done, something was generally spoken or declared.** "Be healed!" "I will: be clean." In some instances the aspect of taking

authority over sickness is predominant, but in others it is an example of *"out of the overflow of the heart the mouth speaks"* (Matthew 12:34). What was in the heart of Jesus regarding healing came from his mouth.

4. Prayer and sometimes prayer and fasting (John 11:41-44; Matthew 17:21; Acts 9:40, 28:8).
5. Anointing with oil (Mark 6:13; James 5:14-15). The significance of oil as a symbol of the Holy Spirit has already been discussed.
6. The use of certain means or substances such as clay or saliva (Mark 7:32-37; Mark 8:22-26; John 9:6).
7. Clothing, in exceptional cases, classed in Acts as *"extraordinary miracles"* (Matthew 14:36; Mark 3:10; Acts 19:11-12; Matthew 9:20-21)
8. The power of the Holy Spirit flowing out to heal (Luke 6:17-19).

Steps to Receiving Healing

Information given in Scripture not only provides us with an indication of what God has undertaken to do in similar situations today, it also provides us an understanding of the principles on which the healing grace of God is given. To these we will now turn.

First step - a desire to get well

One of the first things that Jesus looked for in the sick person was **a desire to get well.** We find Jesus often asking the person who came to him, *"What do you want me to do for you?"* (Mark 10:51), or *"Do you want to get well?"* (John 5:1-8). Where there was an earnest desire to be made well on the part of the sick person, it always brought forth an immediate response (Luke 5:12-13).

Strange as it may seem, it is possible for a sick person to have such an investment in their sickness that they do not really want to lose it.

1. Sickness can be used as a means of:
   a. Evading responsibility and the harsh demands of life, and indulging weakness. Thus the first com-

mand of Jesus to the paralytic at Bethesda was *"Get up! Pick up your mat and walk."* (John 5:8).

b. Manipulating or controlling other people such as family members.

c. Punishing ourselves because of self-hatred.

2. Sickness often encourages self centredness because it focuses so much attention inwards. This inward attention can lead to self pity that is dangerously addictive and a great barrier to healing. Compare Psalm 102:1-7 when the psalmist is sick, with Psalm 103:1-5 when he has been healed.

Psalm 102 has the personal pronouns I, me and my no fewer than 19 times in 7 verses, while Psalm 103 focuses on God as an object of worship and praise in every one of the verses quoted. This is compelling reason for believing that God's will for us is not sickness, but healing and health.

3. Where sickness is chronic **it can become part of the familiar furniture of our life.** Change, even when it is change for the better, is sometimes resisted because it is unconsciously seen as a threat. This is particularly true of mental disorders such as depression, anxiety, and feelings of inferiority; but it can also be true of other chronic or congenital ailments.

4. Finally, the possibility of divine healing is sometimes held on to as a last hope, and the person is unwilling to risk losing that hope by putting it to the test. The crisis of faith is therefore transposed into the future, so that there is at least a measure of comfort in the thought that one day they will be healed.

The risk involved in believing for healing in the present is very real and daunting for such people, and this needs to be understood. What they need is for others to take the burden of faith off them and to believe on their behalf for God to heal them now.

The responsibility to have an earnest desire for healing rests not only on the sick person, but on those close to him: relatives (John 4:46ff; Matthew 15:21-28), friends (Mark 2:1-12), even employers (Luke 7:2-10). It is demonstrated when we are prepared to go to any lengths to get the person healed (Matthew 9:1-8, 9:27-31, 17:21). The delays or failures that we experience when praying for the sick are very often due to the lack of real desire on our part, and the absence of a willingness to pay the price of persistence (Mark 7:24-30). It was this persistence in the Syrophoenician woman that impressed Jesus. *"O woman, your faith is great. Be it as you desire."* (Matthew 15:28 - Berkeley).

Second step - a willingness to deal with hindrances

The willingness to deal with any hindrances that stand in the way of healing is often a measure of our desire for healing. Remember that this applies to those who are praying for the sick as much as it does to those who are being prayed for (James 5:16).

Some of the things which may need to be faced up to include the following:

1. Unconfessed sin (Psalm 31:10, 32:5).

   Guilt is a predisposing cause of much sickness, as in the case of the paralytic in Matthew 9:1-8. Jesus dealt first with the guilt problem and then with the sickness. The man at the pool Bethesda (John 5:12-18), had suffered for 38 years from a complaint that had its roots in a sin problem. When we are closed against the conviction of the Holy Spirit and resist his dealing with our sin, the result is that we are closed against his power to heal us.

2. Anger and resentment (Job 5:2, 18:4).

   These attitudes may not only cause sickness, but when we become bitter about our sickness they can also stand in the way of healing. When we are sick, we can be bitter against people who are well. We can be bitter against our parents and against God (in the case of congenital disease or disability). Bitterness is defiling (Hebrews 12:15), and it shuts God out of the situation, because he cannot come in and heal us if thereby, he seems to justify our bitter attitude.

   If we have been bitter against God we need to repent,

and ask his forgiveness. If we are bitter against people because they have hurt us, we need to forgive them and repent of our wrong attitudes to them. If we have been bitter against our parents, we need to repent and to honour them. Note the context of the commandment -

"Honour your father and mother - which is the first commandment with a promise - that it may go well with you and that you may enjoy long life on the earth" (Ephesians 6:2-3).

Sometimes dealing with resentment and bitterness will be sufficient in itself to result in healing; at other times healing is still needed after the hindrance has been removed.

3. Inner hurts.

When physical sickness is the result of emotional problems, inner healing is generally needed as a prerequisite to physical healing (Psalm 147:3). Because of its importance, this subject will be dealt with in more detail later.

4. Wrong attitudes.

These can inhibit faith and hinder our receiving healing.

 a. Jealousy (James 3:16). Characterised by James as demonic, resulting in disorder and evil.

 b. An unforgiving spirit. This is linked with opening our lives to Satan's power (2 Corinthians 2:10), while on the other hand Jesus links forgiveness with faith (Luke 17:3-6).

 c. Marital discord. Particular emphasis is placed on the need for harmony and understanding between husbands and wives, that their prayers are not hindered (1 Peter 3:1-9).

5. Occult healing or involvement (Matthew 24:24; 2 Thessalonians 2:9-10)

This includes healing by spiritualistic means: colour therapy, divination and other occult practices. In many cases, use of such means to obtain healing merely shifts the problem from the physical to the psychic level. In all cases they are damaging as far as faith is concerned. Occult involvement before conversion may still leave a bondage that needs to be broken, while sometimes people suffer from the effects of occult practices by their parents or grandparents. These bondages can be broken by prayer, after the occult involvement has been confessed and renounced.

6. Unbelief. (Hebrews 3:12)

Just as faith is something sown in our hearts by the Word of God, so unbelief is something sown in our hearts by Satan. It needs to be cleansed away by the Blood of Jesus. Unbelief is made up of disobedience and mistrust of God, and is a sin of which we need to repent. It sometimes astonished Jesus (Mark 6:6), and is linked with hardness of heart towards him (Mark 16:14).

7. An unexamined life (1 Corinthians 11:28-30)

There may be other aspects of our participation in the Body of Christ that are unworthy. This goes much deeper than the manner of participating in the Lord's supper. It includes all that the supper symbolises, that is, our sharing together in his life. Our whole walk as Christians, therefore, needs to be constantly examined.

Third step - seek the keys to the situation

In the healing ministry there will be many cases where healing will be a simple and straightforward manifestation of God's grace and power in response to the prayer of faith. This seems to have been the case in the ministry of Jesus and in the early church, particularly where large gatherings of sick people were assembled and many were being healed (Luke 9:11; Matthew 8:16-17, 15:29-31; Acts 8:5-8). Where the power of the Lord is present, faith has evidence to rest on, and people are readily healed (Luke 5:14-15).

In other cases the situation may be more complex and there may be special factors that have to be taken into account. This seems to have been so with most, if not all, of the individual miracles that are recorded in the Gospels and the Acts of the Apostles. Because of his perfect experience of the Spirit, and therefore his perfect discernment, Jesus moved very surely and confidently in this area. Yet, we also find him seeking for the keys to a situation (Mark 9:20-22,29).

In what follows we will discuss some of the keys that may unlock specific solutions. They express divine principles. We have to discover by prayer, by reflection and discernment of the Holy Spirit, which key or combination of keys applies to any particular case.

1. Faith

Faith is the necessary link between the provision of God and our experience of that provision. Until faith reaches out for it, God's provision to meet our need is real, but only potential. Faith makes it actual.

The following important considerations have to be taken into account as far as faith for healing is concerned.

a. Where a faith response is possible from the sick person it seems that this should be sought. This faith may be:
  i. That God is able to heal (Matthew 9:28).
  ii That God is willing to heal (Matthew 8:2).

b. Sometimes the burden of believing is wholly on the sick person. *"Do you believe that I am able to do this?"* Jesus asked the blind men. *"According to your faith, it will be done to you"* (Matthew 9:28-30).

c. Where faith on the part of the sick person is not possible, or is not there, substitutionary faith on the part of others is effectual (John 4:50; Luke 7:2-10; Matthew 9:2, 15:28).

d. Sometimes the only faith required is that of the person who is praying for the sick (Mark 16:17-18; Acts 3:5-6). This is obviously the case when praying for people who are not christians, for babies, for those who are unconscious, or those who are not present at the time. It is also the case when the gifts of healing are being exercised (Acts 3:6; 28:7-9).

e. Corporate faith can help private faith. (James 5:14-16). On the other hand corporate unbelief can hinder private faith (Matthew 13:53-58). Sometimes it is necessary to remove the sick person from unbelieving surroundings and to minister to him privately, or to remove those with weak faith from the situation (Mark 5:37-40; Mark 8:22-26). This is very important in meetings. People can come mainly to see whether anything is going to happen, in which case they are mere spectators, contributing little faith and probably a measure of scepticism to the situation. Or they can come to make things happen, in other words to be actively involved in their faith and in their prayers. Then the power of corporate prayer can enable the power of God to be released to a far greater degree than may be possible in our individual faith or ministry.

f. Faith is created by the preaching or the declaration of the word and can sometimes be discerned in the sick person (Acts 14:9). It is probably the case that much of our preaching on healing is to quicken faith in the preacher himself, and the purpose of much of our praying is to do the same. The confession or declaration of the word produces faith: *"... faith comes from hearing the message, and the message is heard through the word of Christ"* (Romans 10:17).

g. Faith often needs to be released in a specific act at a specific point in time (Matthew 9:20-21). An impetus or encouragement to faith can be given by:
  i. The touch or grasp of the person ministering (Mark 1:31; Acts 3:7).
  ii. The word of healing or command spoken by the person who is ministering (Acts 9:34, 14:10).
  The person who is praying can impart faith into the heart of the sick person. *"What I have I give to you,"* applies also to faith.

2. Confession

Confession, as we have already seen, is our heart and mouth agreeing with what God says (2 Corinthians 4:13). Often what we have received in our faith will not become manifest until we confess it (John 11:23-35; Mark 5:39).

Confession is the outworking of faith, it is not a substitute for faith. It is not the power of positive thinking, nor is it mind over matter. If we have not received the healing in our faith, confession is untrue and may even be presumption. We also have to persist with our faith statement. *"Let us hold fast the confession of our hope without wavering, for he who promised is faithful"* (Hebrews 10:23 RSV). Just as the confession of our faith deals with doubts and fears regarding salvation, so the same confession deals with symptoms as far as our healing is concerned.

3. Obedience

Sometimes confession takes the form of acting in obedience to the word of healing. To the ten lepers Jesus said, *"Go show yourselves to the priest"*. As they went to demonstrate that they were clean, they were cleansed (Luke 17:12-14). The man born blind went in obedience to wash the clay from his eyes and came back seeing (John 9:6-7). Just as there is a close link between God's words and his works, there is a close link between our faith and our obedience (Luke 17:15-19).

4. The Power of the Holy Spirit

Although all healing is through the agency of the Holy Spirit, there were times in the ministry of Jesus and the apostles when the power of the Spirit was manifestly present in an obvious and dramatic way (Luke 5:17, 6:19; Mark 5:30; Acts 5:12-15).

This power might extend to the person and the clothes of the person ministering, and on occasion could be carried on cloths and aprons to the sick (Acts 19:11-12). The power of the Holy Spirit is thus expected to be demonstrable, and there are times when only such a dramatic manifestation of his presence will meet the need of the moment. This is the *"demonstration of the Spirit's power"* (1 Corinthians 2:4-5) that, for Paul, constituted an essential aspect of fully preaching the Gospel (Romans 15;19).

5. The Word of Authority

Regardless of his awareness of the presence of the power of the Holy Spirit, Jesus always moved in authority. Thus, he was able to command healing and deliverance even at a distance. At times the word is spoken to the sick person, at other times the sickness is rebuked (Luke 4:39) or deaf ears are commanded to be opened (Mark 7:34).

Jesus gave his disciples authority over sickness and demons, and this authority is therefore exercised in his Name (Acts 4:10). We need however to understand the basis of delegated authority. It is much more than merely speaking words or using "in the name of Jesus" as a ritual formula. The basis of authority is clearly demonstrated in the life of Jesus and consisted of:

a. Obedience. In the life of Jesus only one will ruled and that was the will of the Father (John 5:30). All authority flows from the throne of God and is inseparable from the throne. Therefore, authority is only vested in us when we are totally obedient to the throne of God, in other words, when we are like the Roman centurion, "a man under authority".

b. Revelation. Jesus operated on the revelation of the Father's works (John 5:20). Out of the revelation that God the Father was a healing God, Jesus, the Son, went out and did the Father's works. When we have a similar revelation that Christ is the healing Saviour, we will go out and do the same works.

78

6. Crisis or Process

Although most of the miracles of Jesus were instantaneous, this may not always be the case with us. We may need to pray more than once for healing to take place. In Mark 8:22-26 we find Jesus praying twice before a man's sight is completely restored. In James 5:14 *"the prayer offered in faith will make the sick person well; the Lord will raise him up"* allows for a progressive recovery. There are also indications that exorcism was sometimes more than a moment's work. In Luke 11:14 we read that he *"was driving out a demon"*, which indicates a continuous tense.

As we saw in Chapter 5, healing includes progressive or gradual restoration to health, whereas a miracle always consists of healing that is not possible or understandable by other than supernatural intervention.

7. The Fight of Faith

Sometimes we imagine that the miracles of Jesus were entirely effortless affairs. In fact, the reverse is the case. There is ample evidence of the struggle of his will against sickness (Matthew 8:3 - *"I will ..."*), and the involvement of his whole being in securing healing (Mark 7:34; John 11:38). Thus there is also our wrestling against the alien powers that hold the human race in bondage. The ultimate victory has been won by Christ, but dispossession of the enemy is still no light affair.

8. Exorcism

In the individual healings of Jesus, there are six in which the sickness or disability is associated with the presence of evil spirits, or where the problem itself was demon possession.

This subject will be dealt with in more detail later, but note two important points:
1. The presence of demons as the cause of sickness is known by spiritual discernment, not from symptoms. Thus blindness is in some cases the

work of an evil spirit (Matthew 12:22ff), and at other times not (John 9:1-4). The same is true of epilepsy (Matthew 4:24, 17:15), and dumbness (Matthew 9:32-34; Mark 7:32-37).

2. Where the cause of sickness was demonisation, Jesus' response was to cast the demons out. When the deliverance was complete, healing followed spontaneously (Matthew 9:32-34). At other times we find Jesus breaking a demonic bondage first and then ministering healing (Luke 13:10-13).

9. Emotions

There is constant evidence of the compassion that moved the heart of Jesus towards the sick and afflicted (Mark 1:41; Matthew 9:36). It seems also that pain roused an instant response (Matthew 8:6-7). At times this compassion resulted in sovereign acts of mercy as in Luke 14:1-4 and 7:13. At other times the emotion that moved the heart of Jesus was anger against sickness and death (Mark 3:5; John 11:38).

Fourth step - expect the evidence

Although there were times when healing was not immediately manifested, it was always ultimately evidenced. The blind saw, the lame walked, the woman with the haemorrhage *"felt in her body that she was freed from her suffering"* (Mark 5:29). With Paul, scales fell from his eyes (Acts 9:18). Lepers were commanded to go to the priest and demonstrate their healing (Matthew 8:4).

Expectancy is linked with hope. It is the openness to receive. Where there is no expectancy, there is no door open to receive. We will never experience more than we receive. Before we can experience healing we must receive it. But we will never receive more than we are open to. Therefore if we are not open to healing, we will never receive it.

Summary

The biblical accounts of the miracles set out principles of healing that cover every eventuality we are likely to meet: minor illnesses, advanced stages of disease, chronic, congenital and terminal conditions, the result of accidents, psychosomatic disorders and demon possession. Healing may be with the person present or at a distance, and by various means including touch, command, prayer, anointing.

The first step in healing is a desire to get well. It is possible for sickness to be a means of avoiding responsibility and of manipulating people for our own ends. The desire for healing is also necessary on the part of those close to the sick person or seeking his healing.

The second step is the willingness to deal with hindrances to healing, such as unresolved guilt, resentment and bitterness against people, parents or God; a wounded spirit; wrong attitudes such as jealousy or unforgiveness; and occult healing or occult involvement.

The third step is to seek the key to the situation where it does not yield to the simple prayer of faith. Even with faith there are different aspects. Sometimes the faith of the sick person is crucial, at other times it is substitutionary faith on the part of friends or those ministering to the sick person. At times the person ministering has to rely on his own faith, at other times the issue is one of corporate faith or corporate unbelief.

Faith is created by the Word of God, but may need to be released at a specific time and by a specific act. At such times the touch or grasp of the person ministering may become the point of faith.

Healing may be instantaneous or we may need to persevere in prayer to complete the recovery. Prayer for the sick is not effortless. Though the power is God's, we are called to struggle by means of that power against the powers that hold man in bondage. Whether or not the sickness is caused by the presence of evil spirits is a matter for spiritual discernment, not merely by deduction from symptoms. Healing is often spontaneous when the demons are cast out, at other times we may have to first cast out the spirit and then lay hands on the person for healing.

7
Healing the Emotions

There are many people today who are ill, not physically, but emotionally. There are others who are physically sick, but the functional or organic disorders from which they suffer are due to emotional or spiritual disorders. The pain of such emotional disturbances is often more intense and crippling than physical hurt, but is much less easily recognised by others. A broken leg attracts sympathy and consideration the way a broken heart seldom does.

The church has often neglected the area of the emotions as though they were of little concern to God, and had no part to play in christian experience. But the emotions are still there, and if they are not open to God, they will be open in the only other direction available: towards the world, the flesh and the devil. Then we wonder why christians have nervous breakdowns and other emotional problems of varying degrees of severity.

What are the Emotions?

Emotions are feelings or affects (hence 'affections'). Not all feelings however are emotions. Pain, drowsiness and hunger are somatic feelings that alert us to bodily conditions. Emotions are psychic responses to experiences of our inner or outer worlds, thus, a sudden noise may make you afraid, an insult make you angry, or the sight of a person in deep need may cause you to feel pity.

The response that we experience in such situations is accompanied by feelings that may also be the cause of physical changes or sensations. When we are angry we flush and our muscles tense; when we are nervous our mouth dries up and the palms of our hands sweat (Job 4:14-15). The physical sensations of extreme emotional stress are seen in this passage:

"At this my body is racked with pain,
pangs seize me, like those of a woman in labour;
I am staggered by what I hear,
I am bewildered by what I see.
My heart falters, fear makes me tremble;
the twilight I longed for has become a horror to me"
(Isaiah 21:3-4).

The emotions are psychic motors (e-motus from the Latin movere to move). They move us or we are moved by them to action or reaction.

The mind has a very important part to play in our emotional responses. That is, the way in which we respond emotionally to a situation, depends largely on the way our mind interprets it. For example, the physical sensations experienced in falling off a wharf into the water are the same as we experience in jumping off the wharf into the water for a swim. Our emotional reaction to two events will, however, be quite different. If our perceptions are wrong, our emotional reactions may be mistaken; if our perceptions change, our emotional responses may change.

Furthermore, once activated by a set of circumstances, it is possible for the emotional experience to be repeated merely by recalling the situation. We can still feel embarrassed by remembering a situation that caused us to feel ashamed or uncomfortable, even though it took place a long time ago. This repetitive effect - especially when it produces physical reactions - can, in time, produce functional or even organic sickness in the body.

The need to respond emotionally - as well as mentally and physically - to the influences of the environment, is part of the process of growing up. Certain levels of emotional stress or pressure are as necessary as physical effort. This includes unpleasant emotional experiences. By no means all unpleasant emotional experiences are damaging. In fact grief, disappointment, failure, rejection and fear can all provide growth opportunities.

Where, however, the stress is more than the person can successfully cope with at the time, then hurt or damage can take place, often with long-lasting effects.

Evidences of Emotional Hurt

Wounded feelings are not observable in the same way as physical cuts and bruises, although they are just as real. The results of such emotional hurt can show up in a person's behaviour and attitudes in the following common ways.

1. There are strong emotional reactions or responses without there being sufficient circumstances to warrant them. For example, a fearful person can be afraid or anxious over trivial circumstances, even without being aware of why he is afraid.

   "There they were, overwhelmed with dread, where there was nothing to dread" (Psalm 53:5).

2. The actual experience of feelings can be accompanied by excessive pain. For example, the feelings associated with failure are unpleasant for anybody, but for some people they are so extremely painful as to be crippling.

   "My thoughts trouble me and I am distraught
   at the voice of the enemy, at the stares of the wicked;
   for they bring down suffering upon me and revile me
   in their anger.
   My heart is in anguish within me;
   the terrors of death assail me.
   Fear and trembling have beset me;
   horror has overwhelmed me" (Psalm 55:2-5).

3. In some cases, all feelings are repressed and the person seems unnaturally placid, callous or apathetic. It is as though an emotional overload blows a fuse and thereafter little or no feelings of any kind are experienced (Ephesians 4:19; Ezekiel 11:19).

4. Problems in the area of personal relationships, such as domineering or possessive attitudes, or on the other hand extreme dependence. There may be extreme

85

egocentricity, the person is happy only when all the others' attention is focussed on him or adjusted to his feelings. Or there may be oversensitivity or always wanting to please others - an inability to say no to requests or demands. Characteristically there is difficulty in giving or receiving love and affection and an inability to make or keep real friendships.

5. A poor self-image or an inferiority complex. This can come out in many apparently contradictory ways, for example, a very critical attitude towards others, excessive shyness, a constant drive to prove oneself (often misunderstood as pride), a desire to be recognised, or an inordinate fear of failure.

6. A generally pessimistic outlook on life, running all the way from negative talk and attitudes to compulsive thoughts of a gloomy or morbid nature and, in severe cases, to depressive suicidal states.

7. Uncertainty, indecisiveness and extreme procrastination.

8. Lack of order in physical surroundings. Not mere untidiness but a total inability to bring order into the material environment.

9. Fear, particularly of being in situations that will be too much for them.

10. Amoral attitudes; the person will take whatever they want, or will expect to get it, and will not even consider that thanks is required.

11. Often a woman will not want children in her marriage, or will be unable to cope with children when they are older.

12. The Christian with emotional problems often has severe attacks of spiritual doubts or loses assurance of salvation. It is very important in such cases to identify the real nature of the problem. Intellectual answers are of no avail because the true problem lies elsewhere.

Sources of Inner Hurt

1. As we have already seen, traumatic emotional experiences beyond our capacity to handle, cause

emotional wounds (Luke 10:30-36) ("wounds" v34 Gr "trauma"). These may include bereavement, marriage breakdown, job failure, loss of health, accidents or loss of standing or reputation.

2. Even more common is living for long periods under negative conditions of stress such as strife, nagging, heavy authoritarian discipline, and various forms of psychological cruelty. There is a gradual accumulation of stress until the person reaches breaking point.

3. Negative feelings due to failure to attain goals that we see necessary to meet our needs:-

    a. When the frustration arises because we have actually set ourselves unreachable goals, the predominant feelings are those of worthlessness and depression.

    b. If we believe that the goal is reachable, but we are frustrated by external circumstances or other people, the basic emotions are those of resentment, bitterness and aggression.

    c. If the goal is attainable, and the path to fulfilment is reasonably free from interference, but we are stalled into indecision by a fear of failure, our predominant feeling will be one of anxiety.

    d. When we face competing demands that are mutually exclusive, for example, claims on our time by job, family, church and sport, the result will be conflict and anger.

    e. When there are repeated fear stimuli, or a prolonged basic threat to our self concept, for example being in a job or in a class where we are not keeping up with the others, the result will be anxiety.

    f. When our behaviour violates our own inner standards we experience guilt. Guilt can become chronic.

4. Experiences in childhood are often critical because of the extreme vulnerability of the personality in the early years. Feelings of rejection in early childhood can be devastating to some children, and can produce feelings of unconditional badness. A child can feel totally worthless and deserving of only extreme

punishment. Sickness in early childhood, or absence of parents - particularly the mother - can make a child feel very afraid or abandoned. There are also certain especially vulnerable periods in a child's life: beginning at school, shifting to a new district and faced with the need of making new friends, starting high school and college, and problems of adolescence. Critical hurt in these periods is particularly difficult to deal with.

In marriage breakdowns children are the innocent victims. Apart from the insecurity engendered by the break-up of the child's whole world, there is the trauma of finding that the two people he most loves are antagonistic to one another. Trying to resolve the clash of loyalties, the child may blame himself as the cause of the entire problem.

Sometimes it is not what the parents have done, but what they have failed to do. Every child is born with two created needs: the need for love and the need for worth or significance. Parents can meet, or over-meet a child's material needs, but if they fail to meet his or her needs for love or worth, a child may grow up with feelings of rejection and inferiority that can stunt emotional development.

Ability to Handle Stress

The result of stress depends not only on the amount of stress but on the person's ability to deal with it. Our ability to handle emotional stress depends on:
1. The self-concept; the secure person stands up to stress better than the insecure person.
2. Adaptability or flexibility; rigid or inflexible personalities succumb earlier to stress.

Some important qualifications also need to be made regarding childhood experience, otherwise parents can incur undeserved guilt about their parental performance, and children can quite wrongly hold resentful feelings against their parents.

1. The results of childhood experiences on a person's life are almost completely unpredictable. They depend on both the child's personality and his environment. What to one child may be a secure and encouraging environment, may be stifling and repressive to another child of the same family. What to one child is a challenge to which they eagerly rise, is to another a daunting and hopeless struggle.
2. What affects the child is how he interprets the situation, not its objective truth. If a child interprets his father's attitude as rejection or indifference, it will affect him that way, even if, in fact, his father loved him, and was proud of him, and expressed it as well as was possible.

What Happens in Emotional Hurt

The most common result of inner hurt, particuarly in childhood, is that emotional growth is inhibited. We say of such experiences, "I never got over it". It is an accurate description of what happens. We fail to integrate the problem experience, and henceforth it proves an insuperable hindrance to further growth. We may grow up physically, intellectually, socially - even spiritually - but parts of our emotional life are held back in a stage of immaturity. Psychologists are almost unanimous that immaturity stands out as the number one troublemaker in bringing about mental, emotional and social problems.

Feelings of inadequacy, anxiety and depression are often due to facing the demands and stresses of adult life, while part of us - like a small child - feels we cannot cope, or we are never going to make it. Immaturity is also shown in some of our reactions to stress - for example, temper tantrums - or in the inability to sacrifice short-term interests for long-term goals. A child has a very short time perspective, he lives very much in the immediate present. An emotionally immature adult often behaves in the same way.

God's desire for us however, is that: "... *speaking the*

truth in love, we will in all things grow up into him who is the Head, that is, Christ'' (Ephesians 4:15).

Healing for Inner Hurt

We have seen again and again that God's answer to man's need is two fold: the work of the cross and the work of the Holy Spirit. We need to see how this provision meets the problem of emotional hurt and pain.

The Work of the Cross

It is vital for people, suffering the trauma of inner hurt, to understand that when Jesus died on the Cross he dealt with all the damage that sin has done to the human race - not only guilt, but also grief, pain, sickness, despair, fear and alienation. He plumbed the depths of suffering on our behalf.

Jesus suffered spiritually in bearing the judgement of God on sin and evil: he suffered physically - in one of the cruellest forms of execution ever devised - and he also suffered emotionally. In fact, the scripture writers focus more on the shame of the Cross than on its pain.

> *''He was despised and rejected by men,*
> *a man of sorrows and familiar with suffering.*
> *Like one from whom men hide their faces*
> *he was despised, and we esteemed him not.*
> *Surely he took up our infirmities*
> *and carried our sorrows''* (Isaiah 53:3-4).

Jesus knew rejection and hurt beyond anything man has ever been called upon to bear. He came to his own people, to his own beloved city, and they crucified him in the name of the very Father he had come to reveal.

When he died on the Cross, Jesus had lost everything - his ministry, his disciples, his reputation, his privacy, even his own inner integrity because he was made sin for us.

It has been suggested that Jesus on the Cross may have been saying over to himself Psalm 22. It begins with the words: *"My God, my God why hast thou forsaken me?"* It ends in the Hebrew with: *"It is done"*. Verses 11-18 describe in detail the suffering of crucifixion but verse 6 says: *"I am a worm and not a man"*.

Then he found that in the hour of greatest extremity his own Father had turned his back on him. *"My God, my God why hast thou forsaken me?"*

But because Jesus carried our griefs and our sorrows, it means that by his stripes we are healed emotionally as well as physically and spiritually; we are made whole.

The Work of the Spirit

In Romans 8:15 the Holy Spirit is called the Spirit of adoption. This is not adoption in our modern, Western terms. To the Jew, adoption was the entrance of a son into maturity and adulthood. The Holy Spirit is, therefore, the Spirit of maturity to enable us to grow up into Christ (Ephesians 4:15). As part of this ministry he is also the anointing to bind up the broken hearted:

> *"The Spirit of the Sovereign Lord is on me,*
> *Because the Lord has anointed me,*
> *To preach good news to the poor*
> *He has sent me to bind up the broken-hearted,*
> *To proclaim freedom for the captives*
> *And release from darkness for the prisoners"*
> (Isaiah 61:1).

The name that especially describes his ministry, is the one that Jesus gave him in John 14:26: Paraclete, that is, Comforter or Helper.

In order to heal us in our emotions, the Holy Spirit must gain access to them. In other words, we have to open up the hurt areas to his ministry.

91

The Process of Inner Healing

Opening up the Emotions

One of the most important points to remember in connection with inner healing is that you can only deal with a feeling when you are feeling it. Only then have you linked up directly with the hurt and can give God access to it. Look at the diagram below. If I have a will problem, (for example, a bad habit I need to break) I can only deal with it by an act of will, because that is where the problem lies. No amount of reasoning (mind), or remorseful feelings (emotions) get to grips with the real problem. But when it comes to problems in the emotions, the usual response is to push the unpleasant feelings down, and sometimes to bury them so that I no longer feel them. If then, I pray about the problem, all I am in fact giving God is a mental report (+) from my mind, not the feeling (x) in my emotions.

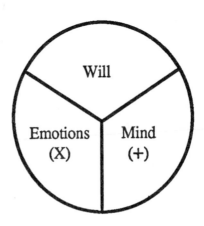

The results of this repression are generally disastrous.
a. We cannot be selective with the feelings we suppress
    Usually we end up burying them all.

b.   Another vital factor in dealing with the emotions is that only feeling can overcome a feeling. The biblical answer to fear, for example, is love (1 John 4:18). When the emotions are shut up tight to keep unpleasant feelings from conscious awareness, they not only shut in the feeling, but shut out the only thing that can heal our hurts, that is the love of God.

c.   The feelings we repress are no longer accessible or under the control of the will. They rage unchecked in the depths of our personality often emerging in the form of sickness or spiritual difficulties.

Remember also, that we are dealing with the present hurt. Sometimes an expression like "the healing of memories" can be a little misleading, by suggesting that somehow we have to go back in time to change something that has already happened. The event that caused the hurt may indeed be years ago - and memory is important - but the hurt is still in the present, and therefore accessible both to us and to God.

Sometimes there is no problem opening up the emotions because the need is so urgent and the feelings so strong. At other times the feelings that are on the surface may not be the real problem, but only the result of a deeper problem; or we may have long-practised defence mechanisms at work to repress unwanted feelings. In these cases we cannot open up the emotions by an act of will. The will it seems can act only to stifle feelings; it cannot produce them. We cannot be joyful, or angry or afraid at will. You will understand this if you have ever tried to laugh at a joke, the point of which you did not see.

Memory is a potent means of opening up the areas of hurt feelings. "*These things I remember as I pour out my soul*" (Psalm 42:4).

One of the particular qualities of the emotions is, as we have seen, that they can be triggered or re-activated by the memory of the situation that originally roused them.

It is here that we need the Holy Spirit to do the searching. Only he knows which memories are significant - and the significant ones may not be the ones we would think are important. Many stressful and even painful experiences, we may have handled totally successfully and profited from them. The critical ones are the ones that were too much for us, and which have been buried out of mind. We need to pray like David:

"Search me, O God, and know my heart; test me and know my anxious thoughts..." (Psalm 139:23).

There are times when a word of knowledge, through the gifts of the Holy Spirit, can uncover to our conscious awareness, circumstances and feelings that we have buried.

In other cases, even the memory of the incident or circumstances may not be sufficient. We may recall the facts and still be unable to come to grips with the feelings. Often the blockage involves wrong attitudes that we have developed. These have to be dealt with before there can be healing. Some of the important aspects are as follows:

a. Resentment or bitterness. While we are holding on to bitterness against people who have hurt us, we effectively lock Christ out of the situation, since he cannot come in and heal us if, by doing so, he would justify our bitterness.

b. Unforgiveness. While we hold on to unforgiveness, we remain under the power of the person or situation responsible for our hurt. We are not free to choose how we will feel or react, even although the persons concerned may be absent or even dead. It is only when we let go of these negative feelings that we can come free from the power of the hurt. When I forgive somebody who has wronged me, I am not saying that the wrong thing he did was right: I am dealing with my emotional reaction towards him. I am letting him go free from the hard feelings I have been holding against him. It is a matter of will. I hold things against a person therefore I can, by my free choice, release him from what I was holding against him. That is why forgiveness is a commandment: it begins with the choice of right behaviour:

"... love your enemies, do good to those who hate you, bless

those who curse you, pray for those who ill-treat you."
(Luke 6:27-28)
c. Grief or sorrow can become a hindrance to healing. In a bereavement, or a broken marriage, or similar relationship, there is a grieving process through which we all must go. But grief becomes idolatrous when it becomes central in our heart and our whole life becomes organised around the memory of our loss. Such an idol has to be cast down.
d. Finally, what we interpret as hurt, may really come from unwillingness or inability to face up to unpleasant truths about ourselves. It is no good trying to forgive the person who spoke the truth to us. The fact is he was right. We were wrong. Truth can wound, but its wounds heal cleanly and quickly if we face up to it.

An honest struggle with issues such as these almost always brings the real hurt and the real issues to the surface so that they are accessible, and we know what we are dealing with.

Handing Over the Hurt to Christ

It is necessary, but not sufficient on its own, for the buried feelings to be opened up. The unique feature of the Gospel that distinguishes it from all forms of human psychotherapy, is that there is a Saviour and a Healer who has taken our hurts, as he took our sins and our sickness, and can make us whole. There are three important aspects to remember.
1. Painful feelings have to be admitted to conscious awareness. No matter how disagreeable or even sinful the thoughts and feelings are, they are part of us - and part of us that God already knows about. Their existence, and even right to be recognised, is vital.
2. We have to let these feelings go to Christ. Jesus identifies with our feelings. It is not only that he himself experienced rejection, abuse and injustice, he also experiences our hurt with us. God who is Love cannot,

it seems, allow a single one of his creatures to suffer without himself suffering with them.

"In all their affliction he was afflicted, and the Angel of his presence saved them; in his love and his pity he redeemed them, and he bare them and carried them all the days of old." (Isaiah 63:9 AV). It is this identification of Jesus with our hurt that makes it possible for us to release into his hands the trauma and hurt we have never managed to cope with.

The purpose in coming to Jesus is not just to experience the feelings all over again; it is to give the hurt over to him. It can go from our heart into the blood of Jesus, the same way as our sins and sicknesses go. For our part, we must be willing to let the hurt go. Strangely, we are often resistant to that. Our problems can become so much a familiar part of our life that we are afraid to be without them. David's psalms are instructive reading. They show a man in touch with the whole range of his emotions, both pleasant and unpleasant, who knows how to pour them out to the Lord.

"Trust in him at all times, O people; pour out your hearts to him, for God is our refuge" (Psalm 62:8).

3. We need to receive the love of God to heal us, and the power of the Holy Spirit - the Spirit of adoption or maturity - to enable us to grow. (Romans 5:5, 8:15).

Because emotional hurt almost always results in immaturity, the healing of the hurt involves a process of growth. In strict terms you cannot be healed or delivered from immaturity, you can only grow out of it. Therefore, while the removal of the blockage, or the healing of the wounds may be immediate, there is usually a time factor involved in growth. Because there is often a lot of life dammed up in these blocked areas, growth can take place very rapidly, but some period of time is always necessary.

Note also that when a major emotional problem has been dealt with, it is not uncommon for the person to temporarily feel quite disoriented. Old familiar landmarks will have disappeared, and for a time there may even be a feeling of being two different persons with an emotional child within us. This is not abnormal, nor is the person in danger of becoming schizophrenic. It is merely that the emotional blockage has been removed and the area of emotional immaturity has been released to grow up. The feeling generally disappears quite quickly.

Even after a problem has been successfully resolved, similar circumstances arising in the future may provoke an instinctive reaction similar to the old one. We have not lost our freedom, it is merely an instinctive "knee jerk" reaction. We need only hand the situation immediately over to the Lord. For example Peter had a problem of cowardice that led him to betray Jesus. It was dealt with by Christ after the resurrection, so that Peter on the day of Pentecost stood up without a trace of fear before the same crowd that had crucified Jesus. But years later when Peter is eating with the Gentile believers and the Judaisers come down from Jerusalem, the old problem catches Peter off balance, he separates from the Gentile christians and Paul has to correct him to his face.

Emotional Growth

Maturing emotionally involves the following:
1. The emotions are continually cleansed and healed from the distortions and hurt caused by sin.

     The emotions are to be purified: *"Create in me a pure heart, Oh God!"* cries the psalmist (Psalm 51:10). In the Bible the heart generally refers to the seat of the emotions. Acts 15:9 tells us that God cleanses the heart by faith. The emotions can be cleansed from the perversion caused by sin, so that they can gradually become what they were intended to be: powerful motivators towards the good, and away from the bad. We are meant to be able to increasingly trust our feelings, to rely on them to motivate us towards God and away from wrong (Psalm 42:1-2, 119:111-113).

2. The emotions are released so that we recognise, accept and respect them as a legitimate and important part of us.

The problem with many people is not too much feeling, but too little. More people have an emotional temperature that is too low, than one that is too high. For many the natural expression of affection and emotion has been almost totally inhibited.

"I will give you a new heart (emotions) *and put a new spirit in you; I will remove from you your heart of stone and give you a heart of flesh* (Ezekiel 36:26). Part of our rights, under the New Covenant, is to receive for our stony lack of feelings a heart of flesh. In other words, we can have the affective side of our nature released and a new set of emotions imparted. Philippians 1:8 tells us that we are meant to experience the emotions of Christ: *"God can testify how I long for all of you with the affection of Christ Jesus."*

3. We learn to guide and correct our emotions from our perception, discernment and understanding. This involves a reinterpretation of our needs. As we have seen, the way in which we interpret situations or events often determines our emotional reaction towards them. Amongst our deepest needs are the need for significance and the need for security. God has already met these needs and he is the only one who can.

Our significance depends on the fact that God loves us and Jesus died for us. We cannot, by achievement, add one iota to that value - nor can any personal failure or lack diminish that value one iota. Therefore, while we may want the approval of others, or want to have success in achieving goals, we do not need them to be eternally significant. Our security depends on the fact that we are eternally held in the hands of Jesus Christ and the hands of the Father.

"I give them eternal life, and they shall never perish; no one can snatch them out of my hand. My father, who has given them to me, is greater than all; no one can snatch them out of my Father's hand" (John 10:28-29).

4. We decide from our understanding and conscience
    what the right behaviour should be and act accord-
    ingly. The energy and drive from the emotions become
    available to power our behaviour. The aim is an easily
    controlled assertiveness. For example the difference
    between being angry and losing our temper is that in
    the former case the energy is channelled, in the latter it
    runs wild. The same is true of fear. Properly handled it
    keys us up to meet a danger; out of control it produces
    a state of panic and disorganised behaviour.

The Fatherhood of God

It seems that we need to know each person of the Trinity
in order to fully experience all that we require for fulness of
life. Consider the symbols used in the Bible:

Holy Spirit - The Hand of God - Meets our need for
power.
The Son - The Head - Meets our need for wisdom.
The Father - The Bosom - Meets our need for love.

It is God the Father who is supremely able to make up the
deficit in our lives of the lack of nurturing care by father or
mother. *"Though my father and mother forsake me"* said
David, *"the Lord will receive me"* (Psalm 27:10). No matter
how unsatisfactory our experience of human fathering has
been, the experience of the Fatherhood of God can totally
meet our needs. No matter how good our earthly father
and mother have been, they are unable to fully meet our
need for unconditional, unchanging love. Only God the
Father can do that.

Summary

The pain of emotional hurt is often more intense than physical sickness or disease, and is often the cause of such disorders. Not all unpleasant emotions are hurtful. They may produce growth responses. But when the stresses are more than the personality can cope with at the time, there can be hurt or damage, so that the emotions either react without sufficient stimulus, cause excessive pain in their experience, or are repressed so that there is little feeling content at all.

Evidence of emotional hurt includes difficulties in personal relationships, a poor self-image, a negative outlook, a lack of feelings, compulsive thoughts and sometimes severe attacks of doubt regarding spiritual truth.

Common sources of inner hurt are traumatic, emotional experiences, long periods of persistent negativity, frustration in attaining goals we see as essential to our fulfilment, and childhood hurts at critical formative stages in our growth.

The result, particulary in the case of childhood hurts, is the stopping of emotional growth so that we face adult life with varying degrees of emotional immaturity.

Inner healing depends on the work of the Cross and the work of the Spirit. On the Cross Jesus bore our emotional pains (griefs and sorrows), while the Holy Spirit is the One who binds up the broken hearted.

The process of emotional healing necessitates the opening up of the emotions to God, the surfacing of buried feelings to conscious awareness, and the handing over of hurts to Christ.

Often wrong attitudes have to be dealt with, resentment and bitterness given away, and people who have wronged us forgiven. It is in struggling with these issues that often the whole hurting mass is brought to the surface where it can be cleansed and healed.

Because the result of such hurt is almost always some form of immaturity, recovery involves a time lapse. Although the blockage can be removed in a moment, growth is a process.

Crucial to maturity in these areas is the understanding that God has fully met our two essential needs: those for significance and security. Crucial to this is the need to experience the Fatherhood of God in order to live as sons and daughters of God.

8
Healing the Human Spirit

We have seen that man is created spirit, soul and body - one person (1 Thessalonians 5:23). When man fell, his spirit was affected first; he died spiritually. Therefore the first application of salvation or healing also affects man's spirit, bringing what was dead back to life (Romans 8:10).

Remember however that in scripture life and death is always a matter of relationship. To be rightly related to God, the source of Life, (made righteous or 'right-wise') is to be alive. To be separated from God is to be separated from Life, and therefore dead. This does not mean however that man's spirit ceases to function. Even unbelieving man has a functioning spirit, but it can relate only to other human spirits or in occultism and spiritism to evil spirit entities, which are also in a state of death or separation from God. Similarly the human spirit of unbelieving man is open to invasion and direction from the devil (Ephesians 2:1).

The Functions of the Human Spirit

The distinctive functions of the human spirit are three in number:

1. Knowledge (1 Corinthians 2:10-16)
    It is our spirit, not our mind that knows. This knowledge is the direct intuitive knowledge we receive from personal experience of another person, or from direct perception or insight. Our knowledge of God, our receiving illumination of spiritual truth, and our personal experience of God, come in this way.

2. Conscience.
   This is the function of the human spirit which -
   a. Passes judgement on our behaviour and attitudes as to whether they are right or wrong. The judgement of conscience on our wrongdoing produces feelings of guilt (Romans 2:14-15).
   b. Bears witness to, or discerns truth (Romans 9:1). Truth is self validating to the healthy conscience. The assurance of salvation, for example, is the witness of the truth of our salvation by the Holy Spirit to our spirit (Romans 8:1).
3. Communication.
   When we are united to another in spirit there is communion or communication. When we reach out to God in our spirit there is worship (John 4:24).

Damage to the Human Spirit

Sin has comprehensively and severely damaged the human spirit in two main areas -
1. In its **functioning** - understanding is impaired, conscience is compromised and responsiveness is inhibited.
2. In its **states or conditions** - it may be troubled, agitated, hurt or broken etc.
We sometimes assume that when we are born again, the work in our spirit is complete and finished. Both scripture and experience prove otherwise. Even when the person has been born again and restored to a living relationship with God through Christ, there may be aspects of his spirit that need correcting or healing. We will consider them first under the functions of the human spirit and then under some common states or conditions.

Damage to the Spirit's Functioning

1. Impaired understanding.
The inability of the human spirit to receive, or its impaired capacity to receive, is described in the Bible

in terms of blindness and deafness. The unbeliever is totally blind and deaf until he is touched by the Holy Spirit. Conviction is opening blind eyes and deaf ears to "see" or "hear" the truth. But a christian can be blind or nearsighted (2 Peter 1:9) or dull and hard of hearing (Hebrews 5:11f).

2. **Spiritual blindness.**
   The blind person is unable to perceive or understand spiritual truth. He may try to grasp it, or even to believe it, but its true significance seems always to be beyond his grasp (2 Corinthians 4:3-4; 1 Corinthians 1:18). Blindness can lead to confusion, deception and perversion (2 Timothy 3:7).

3. **Spiritual deafness.**
   This emphasises particularly the inability to hear the voice of God in a way that brings understanding. The person prays, but there seems to be no response; he reads the Bible or listens to preaching, but it never appears to reach him in a way that confronts him or draws a living response. He finds difficulty with guidance, worship or the gifts of the Spirit.

Blindness or deafness is caused by, or linked with the following:
a. Hypocrisy or pretence (Matthew 23:15-26). Notice the repeated refrain *"You hypocrites ..." "You blind guides"*
b. Sin, if not dealt with, always blunts the spiritual senses (Psalm 38:13-18; Matthew 6:23). In particular note the effect of guilt, disobedience and hatred in desensitising the spirit (Isaiah 59:9-13; 1 John 2:11; Ephesians 4:18-19).
c. Backsliding or an unwillingness to advance in the christian life also impairs the spiritual senses (2 Peter 1:9; Hebrews 5:11-14; Revelation 3:17).
d. Hardness of heart (Hebrews 3:15, 4:7; Mark 8:17). This is obstinacy, an unwillingness to be challenged, reproved or corrected.
e. Ignorance (Romans 2:17-23). There is an ignorance that is to be treated gently (Hebrews 5:1-2), but there is

also ignorance that is wilful and linked with hardness of heart (Ephesians 4:17-19).

f.   Unwillingness to repent (Matthew 13:14-15). For some people blindness and deafness have a moral base, they are deliberately chosen states to protect themselves from the truth.

g.   Demonic darkness or deception (2 Corinthians 4:3-4). All occult involvement, even at a superficial level, brings spiritual darkness. This needs to be specifically dealt with. (See chapter on deliverance).

There is also a **judicial blinding** by God, creating a sleeping or slumbering spirit, when the chosen blindness or deafness is, as it were, confirmed by God (Isaiah 6:10, 29:10; Micah 3:6; Psalm 69:23; Romans 11:8). That is a state alterable only by God.

Compromised Consciences

In its operation the conscience has both form and content. **Form** is the way that conscience works. It tells me **when** I am doing wrong or when I am doing right, by passing categorical judgements on my behaviour.

The form of conscience is universal, that is, conscience works in the same way for everybody regardless of age, learning or culture.

Content is the basis on which conscience makes its judgements. It tells me **what** is wrong or what is right. The content of conscience is variable, it depends on age, learning, background and culture. It changes with conversion and progressively with growth in the christian life.

Damage may take place both in the way that conscience functions and in the content on which it relies for its judgements.

1.   As far as the form or the way it functions is concerned, a person's conscience may be:

a.   Weak (1 Corinthians 8:7-12). The voice or judgements of conscience are feeble and easily disregarded or misunderstood. This is particularly in terms of its ability to be heard before action, rather than after. The conscience is often weak in the case of an immature christian.

b. Wounded (1 Corinthians 8:12). When a weak or immature conscience is faced with a difficult judgement that is beyond its capacity to deal with, it can be wounded or damaged. The conscience becomes uncertain in its judgement or discernment. Moral confusion can result, which is why the over-riding limitation on the behaviour of the mature christian is not his own conscience, but that of the weaker brother (1 Corinthians 8:13).

c. Seared (1 Timothy 4:2). The picture of being cauterised by a branding iron. When the voice of conscience is persistently disregarded over a particular issue, the conscience becomes progressively insensitive and callous in that particular area. Ultimately it may cease to register judgements at all and the person experiences no guilt feelings over behaviour that he knows or acknowledges is wrong.

2. As far as its content is concerned a person's conscience may become:

a. Defiled. That is soiled or stained (1 Corinthians 8:7; 2 Corinthians 7:1; Titus 1:15). The conscience becomes accepting of certain forms of evil and its judgements are corrupted and misleading. Exposure to pornography, or violence on the media or in literature can defile the conscience.

b. Evil or wicked (Hebrews 10:22). Persistence in sin first defiles the content of the conscience and ultimately makes it evil. In this state the judgements of conscience will be at variance with or even the reverse of those that are in harmony with God's law and character. This is the depravity described in Romans 1:28-32.

Inhibited Responses

This occurs when the spirit is **imprisoned or bound.** An imprisoned or bound spirit is evidenced when the person is:

a. **Unable to reach out** to God or to other people. Such a person is shut in on themselves and often does not even know how to reach out or to make contact. There is a deep sense of loneliness or alienation.
b. **Inhibited or incapacitated in making free choices** as far as actions and behaviour are concerned. Often such people are trapped in addictions, enslaving habits or wrong relationships, from which they cannot break free.

An imprisoned or bound spirit may be caused by a number of different conditions amongst which the following are common:

a. **Rebelliousness** (Psalm 107:10-11). The person who is in constant rebellion against God or against legitimate authority is not free, he is in captivity - 'in darkness, misery and chains'. He is turned in on himself in extreme defensiveness that cuts him off from others and inhibits his freedom.
b. **Affliction** (Job 36:8). This may be troubled circumstances, persecution, difficult relationships or sickness of body or mind. Not only can damage in the human spirit affect our health or our circumstances, but, trouble in any of these areas can blind or imprison our spirit.
c. **Occult bondages** (Isaiah 49:9, 24-5; Acts 8:23). A common result of occult involvement is a spiritual bondage that needs to be broken.
d. **Sin.** Besetting or enslaving habits and particularly the more spiritual sins - pride, envy, self pity, arrogance etc (Lamentations 1:14; Hosea 10:10; Isaiah 58:6) imprison the spirit. The same is true of drug or other addictions.
e. **Poverty and need** (Psalm 69:33). There is a poverty of life and spirit as well as a poverty of money or possessions. The bondage of the helpless poor is first of all in the spirit.
f. **Spiritual dryness** (Zechariah 9:11). Every christian goes through times when it seems that the joy and excitement has gone out of our spiritual experience

These are common and temporary experiences, but we can get imprisoned in such waterless pits.

g. **Fear** brings slavery (Hebrews 2:14; Psalm 79:10, 102:20). This is not the fear which is part of our normal emotional endowment in the face of threat or danger, but the existential fear or anxiety which is related to death and the power of the devil. From this we have been delivered.

h. **Legalism** (Galatians 5:1-10). This is the letter of the law that kills (2 Corinthians 3:6). The person caught in legalism is characteristically bound in their spirit.

States or Conditions of the Human Spirit

There are certain states or conditions of the human spirit that cause pain and suffering and need ministry to bring healing. Often we need discernment to distinguish between what is a condition of the human spirit, and what is the presence of an evil spirit, because the symptoms may be very similar.

Note particuarly the following states:

1. **A troubled spirit.** The person's spirit is in a disturbed state that may be due to
   a. Anxiety (Genesis 41:8; Daniel 2:1).
   b. Agitation (John 13:21).
   c. Fear or alarm (Daniel 7:15).
   d. Distress (Lamentations 1:20, 2:1).

   The cause may be stress or pressure in material circumstances or problems in relationships. A troubled spirit needs peace and a wrong discernment that focuses for example on a need for deliverance will make the condition worse.

2. **A fainting spirit.** When the stress in a situation becomes too great the person's spirit can be over-whelmed (Psalm 142:3, 143:4) or despairing (Isaiah 61:3). In other cases disappointment can be so severe as to sap the life of the person's spirit so that it becomes spent or dim (Psalm 143:7; Ezekiel 21:7). A fainting spirit needs reviving and encouragement.

3. **A grieved (hurt) spirit.** This is not only the grief experienced in a loss or bereavement, but the hurt of rejection or rebuff (Isaiah 54:6), or the wounds caused by sarcastic or cutting words (Proverbs 12:18, 18:21; Jeremiah 9:8). The person experiences pain as, or more severe than that caused by a physical wound. A grieved or hurt spirit needs comfort and healing.

4. **A fearful or timid spirit** (2 Timothy 1:7). Fear states can range all the way from vague, formless anxieties to disabling dread and terror (Job 4:13-15). A fearful spirit needs reassurance.

5. **A broken spirit.** This is the most serious condition because suffering and stress has driven the person's spirit past breaking point. He loses the courage to get up again or the will to go on living (Proverbs 18:14; Job 17:1). Sometimes the spirit is stricken down by a calamity (Proverbs 15:13) or crushed under the weight of affliction (Isaiah 65:14) or guilt (Psalm 38:8) or broken by the discovery of having been deceived (Proverbs 15:4). The broken spirit needs to be revived (Isaiah 57:15).

Wrong attittudes of spirit. There are other conditions that are due to wrong attitudes. These states can compound and complicate the other difficulties experienced, and also cause problems on their own. They can often be discerned as lying beneath behavioural or relational problems. Some of these are as follows:

1. **Pride** (Proverbs 16:18; Ecclesiastes 7:8; Daniel 5:20). This is an arrogance or haughtiness that refuses to be opposed or criticised, and rides roughshod over other people's interests and opinions. It is the root of rebellion and is an attitude that God opposes (James 4:6).

2. **Heresy.** This is called a spirit of falsehood (1 John 4:6) or a spirit of harlotry (Hosea 4:12, 5:4). In the Old Testament adultery and harlotry are used of spiritual unfaithfulness. This is a state of spirit that rejects truth and goes after all manner of false and deceptive teaching. It is more than a lack of discernment, it is a

readiness to accept anything other than the truth of God (2 Corinthains 11:3-4).

3. **Deceitfulness** (Jeremiah 9:4-8). Deceit is lying to gain an advantage or to avoid responsibility. A person can so defraud and manipulate the truth that he ends up being self deceived (1 John 1:8; James 1:22). Deceit is literally "a sin against common sense".

Salvation and our Spirit

The needs we have been dealing with are spiritual because they relate to man's human spirit. To meet man's spiritual needs there has to be a spiritual provision and a spiritual means of applying that provision.

The Work of the Cross

The Cross was a spiritual work of grace. Note the significance of the following:

1. The atonement dealt with spiritual problems - sin, sickness and evil spirits.

2. It was a spiritual transaction effected by the Blood of Christ in the heavenly Tabernacle (Hebrews 9:11-14).

3. It was through the eternal Spirit that Christ offered himself unblemished to God (Hebrews 5:14).

4. His blood cleanses our conscience (spirit) from works that lead to death, so that we can serve the living God (Hebrews 5:14).

5. Christ, as the last Adam, is a life-giving spirit (1 Corinthians 15:45).

6. When we are united with Christ, we are one with him in spirit (1 Corinthians 6:17). The grace of Christ is with our (human) spirit (Galatians 6:18; Philippians 4:23).

The Work of the Holy Spirit

The Holy Spirit indwells the human spirit and thereby unites us eternally to Christ the Life (1 John 4:13; Galatians 4:6).

1. It is the Spirit who gives life (John 6:63; 2 Corinthians 3:6; Romans 8:10).
2. He is the anointing who brings freedom for the prisoners, sight to the blind and hearing to the deaf (Luke 4:18; Isaiah 35:5-7).
3. The vehicle of the Spirit is word (John 6:63) the uttered or Spirit-quickened rhema word of God (1 Corinthians 2:13; Ephesians 6:17).

Ministering to the Spirit

Ministering to the human spirit requires first of all confidence that we have been made competent ministers of the new covenant. This is ministry in the spirit and in the Holy Spirit (2 Corinthians 3:6). Therefore the spiritual gifts of discernment, wisdom, knowledge, prophecy and healing are all important. Furthermore we need to realise that the Spirit's anointing and the Spirit-quickened word are ministered only as we use our spirit, and only as we reach the other person in his or her spirit. The human spirit becomes a kind of carrier wave on which the Holy Spirit moves. This dimension of spiritual functioning cannot be overstressed.

A basic approach is as follows:

1. **Identify the area of need.** This may be damage to the functioning of the spirit, or a diseased or damaged condition or state of the spirit. Discernment is needed.
2. **Deal with the question of repentance and the rectifying of wrong or sinful attitudes** such as unforgiveness, bitterness, resentment, hardness of heart etc. Do not rush through this stage. You are dealing with very deep issues, and must be careful of superficial binding up before the real problems have been faced.

"They dress the wound of my people as though it were not serious. 'Peace, peace' they say when there is no peace." (Jeremiah 8:11).

3. **Be open to the revelation and prophetic gifts of the Holy Spirit.** Get a word from God that answers the condition you are dealing with.

4. **Minister into the person's spirit** the healing, liberation, affirmation or life that is needed, until there is a response of faith in the person's spirit to receive it.

5. **Follow up.** New attitudes and responses have to be developed.

   a. Teach the person how to live out of their spirit in all its functions - intuition, conscience and communciation (Isaiah 26:9; Psalm 77:6; John 4:24; 1 Corinthians 14:14-16).

   b. Make sure they are filled with the Holy Spirit and are learning to walk in obedience to him and to the word of God.

Summary

Sin not only separated man from God, it comprehensively damaged his whole being including the human spirit. Even after regeneration restores us into a living relationship with God the source of life, aspects of the spirit still need cleansing, healing and correcting.

The human spirit can be impaired in its capacity to receive knowledge, it can be shortsighted or hard of hearing; its judging faculty, the conscience, can be damaged in its functioning, being weak, or wounded or seared, or it can be defiled or even wicked in content. Similarly the spirit can be bound and inhibited in its ability to reach out to God or others.

Healing for the human spirit is found in the spiritual work of Calvary and in the ministry of the indwelling Holy Spirit in the believer's spirit, He is the anointing that gives sight to the blind, opens deaf ears and brings the captive out of the prison house. In ministering to the human spirit we need the discerning, revelatory and prophetic gifts of the Holy Spirit, we need to deal with the question of repentance and the rectifying of wrong and sinful attitudes and we need to know how to minister into the person's spirit so that they experience the liberation, healing, affirmation or life that is necessary to bring wholeness and growth.

9
Healing from the Demonic: Deliverance

The ministry of Jesus touched the three great areas of human need: sin, sickness and bondage to evil spirits. His commission to the church includes all three. Therefore we are to *"preach the Gospel, heal the sick, and cast out demons"*.

In dealing with the demonic dimensions of human affliction, we need to stay very close to the scriptural revelation in order to avoid two extremes: one that ignores demonic activity altogether, and the other that becomes morbidly fascinated with the evil supernatural, so that demons are seen behind every misfortune and every sin.

The first requirement is for us to understand the true nature of the problem and then to see clearly the provision that God has made for it to be dealt with.

The Devil and his Angels

There is a vast amount of scriptural evidence that the devil is a personal being and not just a symbol of evil or a figure of speech. Satan was created amongst the cherubim, the highest class of angels, and was given the most exalted position in creation. The reason for his fall seems to have been pride and a desire to usurp the very throne of God (Ezekiel 28:12-17, Isaiah 14:13-14). In his fall Satan perverted other angels - perhaps a third of all those created (Revelation 12:4) - so that we read of the demons as the devil's angels (Matthew 25:41), and Satan as the prince or archon of the demons (Matthew 12:24-28).

Characteristics of demons. The following summarises the biblical evidence.
1. Their being
   a. They are spirits, that is, they do not have flesh and blood bodies. They are not normally visible to human eyes, but they can assume visible forms. (Genesis 3:1; Revelation 16:13).
   b. They are genuine persons with intellect, feelings, will and moral responsibility (Acts 16:16-17; Luke 4:33-35, 8:28-31; James 2:19).
2. Their abilities
   a. They have preternatural (more than natural) intelligence, strength and powers (Luke 8:29; Acts 16:16-17; 2 Thessalonians 2:9). Note that we reserve the term supernatural to refer only to the working of God.
   b. They can affect the natural elements. In the stilling of the storm in Mark 4:36-39 it is clear that the storm was demonic. Jesus uses the same words, "rebuke" (epitomao) and "muzzle" or "still" (phimoo), as he used in dealing with the evil spirits (Mark 1:25). They can also affect animals (Mark 5:13).
   c. They can cause sickness (Luke 7:21, 8:2, 13:11).
   d. They are the source of both temptation and torment for man (Matthew 4:2-4; Acts 5:1-5; John 8:34; Hebrews 2:14).
   e. They are not limited by normal barriers or confines of space (Luke 8:30 and 33, 11:24-26).
3. Their nature
   a. They are morally perverted and evil - the enemy of all goodness. Thus they are called evil spirits or unclean spirits (Mark 1:23; Ephesians 6:12). Some are more wicked than others (Matthew 12:45).
   b. They work through deception, often deceiving men as to their true character (2 Corinthians 11:14; Galatians 1:8).
4. Their organisation
   a. They are organised in hierarchies of varying power and authority - described as "rulers ... authorities

... powers ... world rulers" (Colossians 2:10,15; Ephesians 3:10, 6:12; 1 Corinthians 15:24).

b. Some of these have power over places and nations. In Daniel 10:5-13, for example, it is clear that the angel sent to Daniel was opposed by a fallen power of greater authority, and in order to overcome had to call to his aid a higher power still (Michael the archangel). But even Michael, when opposed by Satan himself, could not deal with Satan on his own, but only by divine authority (Jude 9).

5. Their limitations

a. It is important to realise that, as created beings, both Satan and the demons are finite, and therefore limited in location, time, knowledge and power. In particular, their sphere is (moral) darkness and they cannot operate in the (moral) light.

"Everyone who does evil hates the light, and will not come to the light for fear that his deeds will be exposed" (John 3:20).

"He (the Devil) *was a murderer from the beginning, not holding to the truth, for there is no truth in him. When he lies, he speaks his native language, for he is a liar and the father of lies"* (John 8:44).

Therefore when a believer is walking in the light, he is beyond the range of Satan's knowledge. Furthermore, the devil does not know the future, although one of the great demonic deceptions is in the prediction of future events (Isaiah 47:11-14).

b. As far as unregenerate man is concerned, the demons are limited by man's free moral will. When man rebelled against God he did not throw in his lot with Satan but went his own way (Isaiah 53:6). God has also put enmity between man and Satan (Genesis 3:15), and - for the sake of his salvation - God protects even unbelieving man's moral freedom against Satan. Thus, for Satan or the demons to have power over man's life there must be some yielding of his will to them.

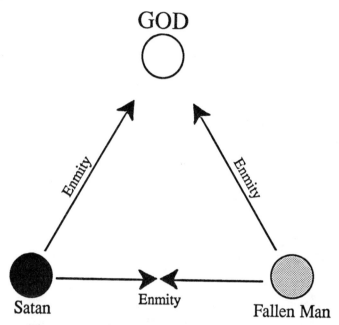

GOD

Enmity

Enmity

Satan

Enmity

Fallen Man

c. The power of the devil and his angels is, in this age, severely restrained by the power of the Holy Spirit (2 Thessalonians 2:7). Only when God permits it, in the final judgements on the fallen earth, will the full hatred of the demons be exercised against the human race without restraint (Revelation 9:1-11).

d. Finally, the power of Satan and the demons was broken at Calvary (John 12:31; Colossians 2:12-15). Jesus is now Victor over all satanic and demonic powers and has vested the fruits of that victory in his church. *"I have given you authority to trample on snakes and scorpions, and to overcome all the power of the enemy; nothing will harm you"* (Luke 10:19).

The Demonic Objective

It seems clear that the fundamental objective of the demons is to gain access to man's spirit. They are spirit beings, but are cut off from God, the source of life, because of their sin. The only other being in the universe who is also spirit is man - and the demons seek to tap into man's spirit to draw life from it.

To gain access to man's spirit they seek man's worship, because worship is a function of the spirit (John 4:24). Thus, the chief form of demonic activity is always essentially religious. This is why the Bible is totally antagonistic to all forms of idolatry, and why the Gospel will have no compromise with pagan religions. The Bible writers knew very well that the gods and idols of the heathen nations were nothing but inert pieces of wood and stone. *"They have mouths, but cannot speak, eyes, but they cannot see"* (Psalm 115:5). But they also knew that behind the idols there was something. Demons are behind all forms of idolatry. *"The sacrifices of pagans are offered to demons, not to God"* (1 Corinthians 10:19-21).

The demonic drive for access to man's spirit is seen even more openly in occultism and the spiritistic religions that abound in the West today. Therefore, while occult involvement may have serious emotional, psychic and other consequences, it is always deadly in terms of faith.

Discernment of the occult dimensions of various meditation and other practices can sometimes be difficult, but three elements seem to be present in all of them, although in different degrees.

1. The paranormal, that is, extra-sensory perceptions that go beyond the traditional five senses. These appear to be human abilities that vastly exceed normal expectations and are possessed by some people to a marked degree.

2. The preternatural. From the paranormal it is a short step to the preternatural in which alien spirit-entities intervene. This is a step that mediums and spiritists easily take.

3. The element of hiddenness or secrecy. The root meaning of the word occult is "hidden". Thus, there are secret societies, esoteric knowledge available only to the initiates, and the opening of the hidden future to the special few with mediumistic abilities or second sight.

This element of hiddenness is a characteristic evidence of occultism, and is found in all cults, in dramatic contrast to the openness and public character of the gospel. As Paul said to Festus: *"It was not done in a corner"* (Acts 26:26).

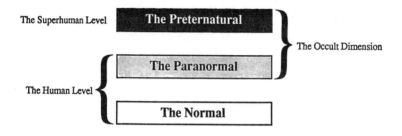

Taken from Principalities and Powers by John Warwick Montgomery published by Bethany Fellowship 1973.

Where Satan and the demons cannot obtain man's worship, they will try to get his service - either knowingly or unknowingly - in order to accomplish their purposes (2 Timothy 2:26; John 8:44; Ephesians 2:1-2). This they will seek to do by deception, by manipulation, by the seduction of power and by playing on fallen man's greed, fear and ambition (James 3:14-15). The strenuous attempts of demons to corrupt the truth are seen today in the appalling confusion of modern cults and heresies (1 Timothy 4:1).

Along with this - and when all else fails - they will try to hold man in bondage to fear, sickness and enslaving habits, and to blind his mind from the truth of the Gospel (Hebrews 2;14; Acts 10:38; 2 Corinthians 4:4; 2 Timothy 2:25-26).

Forms of Demonic Domination

From scripture there appear to be two acute forms of demonic domination (the New Testament term is "demonised") one of which is internal often called possession, and the other external called bondage. Two examples will make the distinction clear.

The demonised boy, in Mark Chapter 9, is an example of possession. Jesus rebuked the spirit and commanded it to come out. On the other hand, the woman with a sickness caused by a spirit, in Luke Chapter 13, is an example of bondage. Jesus broke the bondage and declared her free, and then laid hands on her and healed her. There was no casting out of a spirit.

Demonisation as Possession

From the gospel records we learn that possession occurs in a number of ways -

1. **Involuntarily,** for example, by inheritance or through occult experiences, occult healing or occult curse. In two instances in the Gospels, children were affected: the epileptic boy (Mark 9:21) and the Syrophoenician woman's daughter (Mark 7:25). These cases seem to be linked to inheritance and, at least in the latter, to idolatry or pagan religion. It is worth noting that in Deuteronomy 5:8-9 the judgement regarding *"punishing the children for the sins of the fathers to the third and fourth generations,"* is directly in the context of idolatry. *"You shall not make for yourself an idol"*. This may also explain why the Gentile christians in the early church were warned against knowingly eating things offered to idols (Acts 15:20; 1 Corinthians 8:7).

2. **By invitation,** either knowingly (in the case of those who deliberately give themselves to Satan worship), or sometimes unknowingly (in the case of spirit mediums). For "medium" you can substitute "demonised" man or woman.

    It seems clear that the acute demonic attack, such as

we have described above, has involved at some stage the opening of a human will to demonic power, although it may not always be the will of the person who is afflicted; children, for example, may have been opened to demonisation through the actions of their parents.

3. Possession may be temporary (Matthew 12:43-45), or permanent as in the case of Gadarene demoniac. It may be manifestly obvious, or it may be hidden until the presence of Christ brings a disclosure, as with the man in the synogogue who had an unclean spirit (Mark 1:23-25).

Effects of Possession

The characteristics of the severe form of demonic domination include some, or all, of the following conditions.
1. Personality changes, or a clouding of consciousness (Mark 9:26).
2. Another personality speaking through the afflicted person (Luke 8:28-30).
3. Preternatural strength (Luke 8:29).
4. Preternatural knowledge, and psychic or occult powers (Acts 16:16-17).
5. Severe physical disturbances, for example, epileptic convulsions (Mark 1:26), deaf-mutism or blindness (Matthew 12:22-30, 9:32-34).
6. Suicidal and self-destructive tendencies (Mark 9:22, 5:5).
7. Reaction to, and fear of Christ or his name (Mark 1:24).

Can a Christian be Possessed?

The question is often asked whether it is possible for a Christian to be demonised to this extent. From the scriptures this appears to be very unlikely.

1. Although there is much evidence of the casting out of evil spirits in the ministry of the early church, there is no instance recorded of this ever taking place to a believer. There are ample grounds for believing that it often happened at conversion (Acts 8:5-8).
2. In none of the epistles does possession by evil spirits appear as a danger to which christians are exposed. We are opposed by, and struggle against the devil, the principalities and powers; but we are never warned of the likelihood of being possessed by them.

   The most that can be said is that it ranks with the possibility of apostasy (Hebrews 6:4-6; 10:26-31; 1 Timothy 4:1-3). We must assume that if a person deliberately and finally turns from God to this extent, then demonisation is also possible. For the christian walking with the Lord, however, it is not a condition that is a real possibility.

Demonisation as a Bondage

There are states of demonic domination in which there is no taking over of the personality by an alien being but, nevertheless, there are parts of the person's life where he is enslaved and cannot get free by the ordinary means of grace. Demonic bondage can also be a factor in some sicknesses as with the woman in Luke Chapter 13, and possibly, Paul's thorn in the flesh (2 Corinthians 12:7).

Causes of Bondages

Demonic bondages of this type can apply to Christians. The following predisposing conditions can be found in scripture.
1. **Past occult involvement** creating a blindness or deadness, total or partial, regarding spiritual truth. Simon the magician was converted and baptised when Philip preached in Samaria, yet he sought to purchase from the apostles the authority to impart the Holy Spirit.

Peter's discernment of his condition was, *"I see you are in the gall of bitterness, and in the bondage of iniquity"* (Acts 8:9-23 - ASV).

2. **Habitual transgression in certain specific kinds of sin** can lay the believer open to demonic bondage, for example:
   a. Unforgiveness (2 Corinthians 2:10-11).
   b. Spiritual deception (1 Timothy 4:1-2) and legalism (Galatians 4:9).
   c. Pride (1 Timothy 3:6-7).
   d. Sensuality (1 Corinthians 7:5; Jude 1-10; 2 Peter 2:9-15).
   e. Blasphemy (1 Timonthy 1:20).
   f. Rebellion and stubbornness (1 Samuel 15:23).
   g. Fear (Hebrews 2:14-15).

3. **Often bondage is associated with the flesh** on which the demons capitalise. The works of the flesh include, for example, idolatry, sorcery, and heresy or factions along with other spiritual as well as sensual sins. But if the flesh is dealt with through the Cross (Galatians 5:24), the grounds for demonic domination are broken and freedom often follows automatically.

4. **Bondages can be the result of a curse.** The vehicle of spirit is word, therefore words can be the means whereby life or death, good or evil, blessing or curse can be effected (Proverbs 18:21).

   A curse consists of spirit laden words that bring down evil on those against whom it is spoken (Numbers 22:6, 23:7; Deuteronomy 11:26-28; Judges 5:23).

   Where critical or demeaning words are spoken that articulate things the person who hears them already fears, they can also become a curse (Proverbs 26:2).

The Defeat of the Devil and his Angels

To move confidently and effectively in the ministry of deliverance, we need to understand clearly the nature of Satan's defeat at Calvary, and the grounds on which the demons can be expelled from people's lives. The scriptural basis can be summarised as follows:

1. In the fall man lost his God-given dominion mandate over the earth (Genesis 1:26; cf 3:7-9).

2. The devil usurped control over the world. The ruler (archon) of the demons became the archon of the kosmos (John 14:30; 2 Corinthians 4:4; 1 John 5:19).

3. Thus the principalities and powers are controlled by the devil and his angels (1 Corintians 2:6; Ephesians 6:12) who also foster man's rebellion against God (Ephesians 2:2).

4. Jesus conquered and defeated Satan (Matthew 4:1-11; Acts 10:38) and the demons (Matthew 12:28) and by his ultimate obedience recovered man's dominion over the earth (Philippians 2:5-11; Hebrews 10:11-13).

5. On the cross Jesus destroyed the devil's right or hold over the new creation (John 12:31, 16:11). The devil's power was the power of death; but death had no claim on Christ. His death disarmed death (Hebrews 2:14).

6. This also affected the principalities and powers who were likewise disarmed (Colossians 2:15; 1 Peter 3:22;) *"The rulers of this age who are coming to nothing"*. (1 Corinthians 2:6).

7. Now all authority in heaven and on earth belongs to Jesus Christ (Matthew 28:18).

8. Christ has given this authority to be exercised through the Church (Luke 10:19; 1 Corinthians 2:8; Romans 16:20).

Using the Name of Jesus

Demons are subject to the Name of Jesus (Luke 10:17; Acts 16:18) but using the name of Jesus is not a kind of magic formula - as the seven sons of Sceva discovered (Acts 19:13-16). The Name of Jesus expresses his authority, as he came in his Father's name, that is, with his Father's authority.

Authority is delegated power, therefore, we find that in the ministry of Jesus:

1. The power resident in the Father is now in the Son. *"For just as the Father raises the dead and gives them life, so the Son also gives life to whom he pleases to give it"* (John 5:21).
2. The authority resident in the Father is now in the Son. *"For as the Father has life in himself so he has granted the Son to have life in himself. And he has given him authority to judge because he is the Son of Man"* (John 5:26-27). When Jesus spoke, he spoke with authority. He cast out the spirits with a word, that is to say, with the authority resident in him, he used the power (of the Spirit) resident within him, and demons were expelled (Luke 11:20-22).

In John 20:21 Jesus said to the disciples, *"As the Father has sent me, I am sending you."* As Jesus was sent in the Father's name, he has sent us in his own name so that:

1. The authority resident in Jesus is now resident in us (Luke 10:19).
2. The power (of the Holy Spirit) resident in Jesus is now resident in us (Acts 1:8).

Conditions for the Exercise of Authority

There were two conditions fulfilled in the life of Jesus that have also to be fulfilled in us, so that we can exercise the authority of his name:

1. Obedience (John 5:30). In the life of Jesus there was only one will, the will of the Father. Authority is conditional on obedience.
2. Revelation (John 5:19-20). Jesus "saw" by revelation (insight) what the Father was doing, and out of that revelation he did the same things. Jesus said that we would do the same works as he did (John 14:12), but that involves us also "seeing" what the will of God is, and acting out of that revelation.

    Where there is obedience to the will of God and to the revelation of his word, the power of the Holy Spirit operates through the spoken word, which becomes the word (rhema) of power. It is because of this power in the word, that even the preaching of the gospel can bring deliverance (Acts 8:7-12).

The Process of Deliverance

The casting out of demons and the breaking of demonic bondages is the work of God through the power of the Holy Spirit. It is a sign of the presence of the Kingdom, a demonstration of the power and lordship of Christ over his world.

Casting out Evil Spirits

The afflicted person must desire to be free. As much as a person is able, there must be a sincere repentance and a turning towards the Lord for deliverance. The extent to which this is possible will vary from person to person; but even in the most extreme cases there always remains a measure of moral freedom that must be exercised on the side of deliverance and against the demonic enslavement. If a person does not will to be free, little if anything can be done.

Note the following stages that are generally involved in deliverance:

1. **Binding the demons** (Matthew 16:19). This means forbidding the exercise of their powers and commanding them to harm no one. In some cases it may mean forbidding them to speak. *"No one can enter a strong man's house and carry off his possessions unless he first ties up the strong man. Then he can rob his house"* (Mark 3:27).

2. **Commanding the demons to come out** (Luke 4:35). Even though demons are spirits, they are spatially located and need to be expelled. Note also, the necessity for the vacuum so created to be filled. The person delivered should be prayed for, to be filled with the Holy Spirit (Luke 11:24-26).

3. **Commanding the demons not to re-enter** (Mark 9:25), and ordering them to go somewhere else. We do not have authority to cast demons into the abyss or into hell. We should therefore, hand them over to the sovereign power and authority of the Lord, to go to the place of divine appointment.

4. **Sometimes there will be struggle and resistance on the part of the demons.** It seems from the Gospel record that in the ministry of Jesus there were times when deliverance was not instantaneous (see Luke 8:29 and 11:14 where the verbs are in the continuous sense). Where there is opposition, it requires the steady persistent exercise of authority in the name of Jesus until the resistance ceases. Remember also that the word of God is the sword of the Spirit and should be declared against the powers of darkness.

5. **Deliverance, is often accompanied by manifestations.** These may include convulsions, loud cries, collapse or somnabulistic states (Luke 9:42; Mark 7:30 margin; Luke 4:33-35). The gift of discernment is important, not only in discerning the presence of evil spirits, but in confirming that the person is free (Mark 9:26-27).

6. **Sometimes healing is necessary after the deliverance;** at other times deliverance means the rapid disappearance of physical or psychological conditions that were the result of demonisation (Matthew 9:32, 12:22).

7. **There may be special keys in each situation** as in the case of healing. For example, Jesus asked the name of the demons in the case of the man possessed of a legion (Mark 5:9). The surrender of the demon's name is sometimes the disclosure of the source of their power. At other times, a knowledge of the origins of the infestation may be important, as in the case of the epileptic boy (Mark 9:21 and see verse 29). There are also cases when special prayer and fasting may be a necessary preparation; and in others there may be a particular demand on faith (Matthew 17:20, 21 - margin).

Similarly the time when action is to be taken may be a significant factor (Acts 16:18). Deliverance, as with

healing, can be done at a distance if necessary; and the importance of substitutionary faith, where the person who is afflicted is not in a position to believe, should not be overlooked (Matthew 15:21-28).
8. Finally, **follow-up** in counselling and prayer support is very necessary to establish the person in his freedom.

The Breaking of Bondages

Where there are bondages in a Christian's life, the following steps are important:
1. Repentance and confession of sin that is involved in the bondage. Something more than repentance and confession may be necessary for freedom, but this first step is essential. No bondage frees us from taking moral responsibility for our failure and sin.
2. Recognition of the source of the problem as demonic in nature. Not all sin problems - or even many of them - are of this nature; therefore discernment is necessary. But a sin or habit that does not yield to other means may have demonic aspects. Discernment of the demonic source of a problem may also apply to a physical ailment (Luke 13:11-16).
3. A person is not forgiven from a bondage or healed of it - the bondage is to be broken by command in Jesus' name (Matthew 16:19). We are to speak the word of authority that snaps the chain and cuts the link with demonic power. The power behind the word is the power of the Holy Spirit. It is the anointing of the Spirit that breaks the yoke of bondage. Note the action of Jesus in Luke Chapter 13. First, he broke the bondage, *"Woman you are freed from your sickness"*; then he laid his hands on her and healed her.
4. Often the word of prophecy is important in declaring the person free.
5. Restructuring life-style, particularly the thought life, is vital. Self discipline, the renewing of the mind, and the cultivation of praise are all important.

Occult Enslavement

This is becoming a very common factor to be dealt with. Out of ignorance, many Christians have become involved in various occult practices; or they have taken part in various forms of magic, spiritism, divination or Eastern meditation techniques before they were Christians. The effect on the individual depends on the depth of his involvement and also on the degree of spiritual sensitivity in the person.

Involvement in occult practices may also produce effects in later generations, even although they themselves may not have directly participated in such things. The effects of occult enslavement include apparitions, voices, extreme fear, and widely varying psychic, emotional and physical effects. The most common (and almost invariable) characteristic is, however, great deadness or blindness in terms of spiritual truth - an inability to experience the Holy Spirit, difficulty in faith, unreality in prayer and so on. This may be on its own or may accompany other symptoms.

In counselling persons with occult problems, settle the following points with them:

1. A full conviction and confidence that only Jesus Christ can set them free.
2. Confession of the occult involvement as sin, and repentance from it (Leviticus 19:26,31; 20:6,27; Deuteronomy 18:10-12).
3. The person should verbally renounce the occult practices in the name of the Lord. This renunciation must be total and unequivocal.
4. Anything that had to do with the practices should be destroyed: books, objects, charms and so on (Acts 19:18-19).
5. The counsellor should declare the assurance of forgiveness and then break the bondage in the name of Jesus. As in deliverance, the breaking of a bondage is the destruction of a real demonic hold on the life. Either the bondage is broken, or it is not; the person praying must persist until the chain breaks. Usually

there will be an experience of release and freedom that is sometimes quite dramatic. Discernment is often necessary to know when the job has been done; and, again, the prophetic ministry has an important part to play in bringing the word of the Lord that declares the person to be free.

6. Follow-up and prayer support is essential to establish the freedom and consolidate the person in his new walk.

The Deliverance Minister

It needs to be understood that deliverance is an actual battle with real, malignant foes. We are to wrestle against them and overcome them by the Blood of the Lamb and the word of our testimony; we must never take the fight lightly.

Aspects that are of particular importance for the person ministering are these:

1. Humility and obedience.

    "Submit yourselves, then to God. Resist the devil, and he will flee from you" (James 4:7).

    Pride and self-reliance negate our effectiveness in the deliverance ministry and may bring us into danger.

2. Knowledge and appropriation of our spiritual armour (Ephesians 6:10-18). The armour of God is a set of conditions God wants to establish in our life that will prevent Satan from working and will enable God to work. These life conditions are truth, righteousness, peace, faith, hope and the Spirit-quickened word of God.

3. A living faith in the victory of Calvary expressed in the Blood of Christ, and confidence in the authority vested in the resurrected and ascended Lord Jesus, are all-important.

4. A disciplined life. If there are areas of manifest failure and weakness in our own life, we will never be able to move with authority against demonic powers that capitalise on these particular weaknesses in the person we are seeking to deliver. A person whose own thought life is impure, for example, can never cast out an unclean spirit.

Summary

Demons are the fallen angels who followed Satan in his rebellion. They are spirits but are beings with intellect, feelings, will and moral responsibility. They are morally evil and seek to oppose God and his people. They have preternatural strength, intelligence and power and are organised in a hierarchy that dominates the fallen world system.

Nevertheless they are finite creatures, limited in space, time, power and knowledge. They cannot overwhelm man's free will and therefore need the yielding of his will to take control. They seek for man's worship in order to tap into his spirit. Failing that, they strive to use man to serve their ends in the world, or seek to dominate, afflict, tempt and spiritually blind him.

Demonic attack is primarily idolatrous in its approach, although it may use other methods. In acute stages it is either internal domination (possession) or external domination (bondage). The former is characterised by personality changes in the victim with another personality or personalities taking over; preternatural strength and knowledge; severe physical and psychological disturbance; destructive, suicidal tendencies; and reaction to and fear of Christ.

Bondages consist of areas in the life where demons can control or manipulate the life. The person is not free, and has fear, depression, compulsive habits or similar problems. The ministry of deliverance is equally effective in either area, but with bondages, because they are associated with the flesh, adequate dealing with the latter often deals with the demonic automatically.

Jesus has conquered Satan and his angels and has given his authority to the Church over all the devil's abilities.

The power resident in Christ (the Holy Spirit) is now resident in us. The authority resident in Christ is now resident in us by his name.

The conditions for the exercise of this authority are obedience and revelation. One will - Christ's One work - his.

Demons are cast out by command in Jesus' name. They should be commanded not to harm anyone, to come out, not to re-enter and to go to the place of divine appointment.

Bondages require confession of the sin, recognition of the demonic content of the problem and loosing in the name of Jesus. In occult involvement there needs to be confession of the involvement as sin, and renunciation by the person involved. The bondage can then be broken, and the person set free.

The person involved in deliverance ministry needs to understand and appropriate the armour of God and to maintain a life of personal holiness.

10
The Healing of Relationships

Broken or stressed relationships represent one of the most difficult areas of human need. It is also one in which the results from christian counselling are often most disappointing. Some of the reasons for this are:
1. We have failed to study the basic biblical groundplan for human relationships. Unless we know this, we cannot correctly identify departures from the plan, or the steps that are needed to restore divine order.
2. We have generally lacked a sound biblical model of reconciliation, and have been left with little more than the insights of psychology and group dynamics. The results of these are singularly unimpressive.

The Nature of Relationships

Definition:
A relationship is the mutual sharing of life or some aspects of life, between two or more persons.

From this definition two important consequences follow:
1. **A relationship is mutual,** that is, each party contributes something to it. The contribution need not be the same on both sides, for example, a workman contributes his labour, the employer contributes a salary or wages. Nor does the contribution need to be equal on both sides. But if there is not some mutual contribution there is no relationship. (1 Samuel 18:3-4; Genesis 29:14-20). Furthermore a broken relationship can be reconciled only if there is the mutual desire for

reconciliation. It cannot be reconciled unilaterally.
2. **A relationship is a separate factor** alongside the individuals who make it up. In a marriage there are three factors.
   a. The husband
   b. The wife
   c. The husband/wife relationship

   This explains why you can have two very ordinary, not very gifted people, and yet a marriage relationship that is rich and growing. On the other hand you can have two quite gifted and talented individuals with a threadbare marriage. The difference is not what each has, but what each is putting into the relationship. Again, problems inevitably arise in a relationship like a marriage when a wife, instead of working on the wife/husband relationship is working on her husband or a husband is working on his wife.

Relationship Categories

All relationships are grounded on the biblical revelation of man as a being made in God's image. Man was created with both the capacity for and the need for relationships. We are involved in a whole network of them - husband/wife, parent/child, brother/sister, teacher/pupil, master/servant, doctor/patient, supplier/customer and so on. All these relationships can be described or differentiated in the following ways:

1. **By their nature.** Relationships are either,
   a. **Consummatory,** that is a sufficient end in themselves. Man is a social being who forms relationships for their own sake. It is 'not good' for man to be alone. (Genesis 2:18,24).
   b. **Instrumental,** that is, a means to an end. Man is co-operative being who is given a mandate to fill the earth and subdue it. (Genesis 1:28).

Note:
   i   Some relationships, such as friendships are mainly consummatory; others such as work relationships

are mainly instrumental. But both aspects are found to some degree in most relationships. Work, for example, is a social necessity as well as a co-operative undertaking.

ii Different understandings or expectations regarding the nature of the relationship create potential problem areas. If a salesman targets his friends as customers, they will feel they are being "used"; if an employee expects his boss to pander to all his moods, he is likely to be soon out of a job.

2. **In terms of intimacy,** that is the degree of personal closeness involved in the relationship (Proverbs 17:17, 18:24; Genesis 2:23; John 15:13). Marriage or family relationships are more intimate than those between teachers and pupils or between business colleagues. The greater the degree of intimacy, the more painful is a breach in the relationship, whether caused by disagreement or death (Psalm 41:9; 2 Samuel 1:17-27). Differing expectations as to the intimacy of a relationship, if not expressed or understood, can be a fruitful source of problems. One party expecting a high degree of intimacy, may be perceived by the other as demanding or intrusive; the other person may be seen for his part as distant or stand-offish.

3. **In terms of scope,** that is, the amount of the party's life involved in the relationship. Intimacy and scope are quite different. A profession or vocation taking a large area of a person's life may not involve any great degree of intimacy. On the other hand, a relationship of strictly limited scope and time, such as that between doctor and patient, or counsellor and counsellee, may involve very intimate matters.

Differing expectations regarding the scope of a relationship can also cause difficulty. A wife, for example, may expect that the marriage relationship involves sharing everything, including what happens at the husband's office. If the husband does not share what goes on at work, she may feel rejected or shut out of an area of his life. The husband, for his part, may see no reason for bringing his office problems home every night, knowing that by tomorrow half of them will cease to be problems anyway. He may think his wife's questions show that she does not trust him. The problem really is that the question of scope has not been talked out and mutually understood.

The Elements of Relationship

All relationships are built on four elements - love, trust, respect and understanding. These elements may be expressed differently in different relationships. Love between husband and wife differs from love between friends. Similarly the dominant factor may differ in different relationships. Trust is probably the major issue in relationships between employer and employee; understanding is probably the major issue in relationships between teacher and pupil. However, all four elements need to be adequately provided for in every type of relationship.

Love includes care (1 Corinthians 12:25), liking, kindness (Ephesians 4:32), romantic attraction, affection, service (1 Peter 4:10), attention, compassion and generosity. (See John 13:4, 15:12,17; Romans 12:10, 13:8; 1 Thessalonians 4:9; 1 Peter 1:22, 4:8; 1 John 3:11, 4:7).

Note

a. In the marriage relationship the biblical injunction to love is given primarily to husbands (Ephesians 5:25; Colossians 3:19). Wives are responders. If they are loved, they will usually find it easy to love in return.

b. Love is the most rugged and most enduring of the four elements. (Song of Songs 8:6-7; 1 Corinthians 13:13). It survives long after the others have succumbed. Sadly, the vulnerable person is the one who can no longer trust or respect the other party in the relationship, but still loves them.

Trust includes confidence in, (Proverbs 31:10-12; 2 Corinthians 7:4,16, 8:22); loyalty, honesty (Colossians 3:9; Zechariah 8:16); faithfulness (1 Corinthians 4:2);

reliability; capability; courage; dependability and consistency. (See Exodus 14:31; Titus 2:9-10).

Note

a. Trust may take time to establish - trustworthiness may need to be proved - or it may be a step of commitment, as when someone is appointed to a position of trust.

b. Trust is a critical element in the relationship between leaders and those they lead. Any personal moral failure in a leader is also, whatever else it is, a breach of the trust his people have placed in him.

c. Trust is the most fragile of the four elements. Once lost, it is very difficult to restore (Acts 15:38). Restoration always takes time. Forgiveness may be the work of a moment, but to restore trust is a much longer process.

Respect is the acknowledgement of a person's worth or value. It includes honour (Romans 12:10), interest in, regard for, recognition, receiving, admiration for and affirmation (See Ephesians 5:33, 6:2; James 2:8-9; Philippians 2:3; 1 Timothy 5:17, 6:1)

Note

a. We are commanded to honour God, our parents, employers, elders, our leaders and one another. When I honour those whom God has given me, I realise how rich my life is. When I neglect to do so, or dishonour them, I impoverish my own life.

b. In marriage the wife is to respect her husband (Ephesians 5:33) and the husband is to respect his wife (1 Peter 3:7). Marriage is to be held in honour by all (Hebrews 13:4). Many things in life today erode our self confidence and self respect. Husband and wife can shore up each others' self confidence, or devastate it more effectively than anyone else.

c. Respect or honour is the element most often overlooked today. Undoubtedly there is a direct correlation between the low self image and lack of self respect endemic in modern society, and society's lack of respect towards God, parents, authority and other people's rights.

Understanding. This involves knowledge, empathy, listening, openness, self disclosure, sympathy, encouragement, insight, communication and discernment. (See Philemon 21; 1 Thessalonians 1:3-4; Revelations 2:2-9).

Note

a. Understanding is the factor that takes longest to build. Next to the mystery of knowing God, is the greatest mystery of knowing another human being. Just as we cannot know God apart from revelation, we cannot know a person apart from his self disclosure.

b. The first thing a person hungers for is to be understood. He does not necessarily want to be agreed with or even approved of, but he does want to be understood. That requires first and foremost that we learn to listen.

c. The deepest level of sexual union in marriage is linked with 'knowing' (Genesis 4:1).

The Breakdown of Relationships

Relationships come under stress when there is persistent failure in meeting one or more of the basic requirements; they break down when those failures remain unresolved.

Typical failures are as follows:

1. Things that wound love or make love difficult

a. Cruelty; physical or psychological.
b. Dislike
c. Rejection
d. Withdrawal or coldness
e. Ingratitude
f. Envy or jealousy
g. Meanness
h. Neglect or indifference.

2. **Things that break trust or make trust difficult**

a. Betrayal or breach of confidence
b. Disloyalty or unfaithfulness
c. Dishonesty or untruthfulness
d. Unreliability
e. Inconsistency, moodiness
f. Carelessness, thoughtlessness
g. Moral weakness or inability to withstand pressure.

3. **Things that damage respect or make respect difficult**

a. Failure, inadequacy or incompetence
b. Irresponsibility and selfishness
c. Criticism, nagging and fault finding
d. Dishonouring, embarrassing or putting down in front of others
e. Pettiness
f. Domination, manipulation or using for own ends
g. Being ignored or disregarded.

4. **Things that cause misunderstanding or make understanding difficult**

a. Lack of communication or inadequate communication
b. Secretiveness, shyness, reserve
c. Feelings of inferiority
d. Bias, prejudice and dogmatism
e. Self deception
f. Insensitivity
g. Inability or unwillingness to listen effectively
h. Cultural or personality differences
i Mistake, misconception and miscommunication.

The Effect of Relationship Breakdowns

When relationships break down we can suffer or be affected in mind, emotion and will.

1. **In our mind, the results may be**

a. Self justification, recrimination, excuse (these are conscious).
b. Rationalisation or other defence mechanisms (these are unconscious).
c. Puzzlement or confusion.

2. **The effects on our feelings may include**
    a. Hurt, sadness, loss, loneliness or depression.
    b. Resentment, bitterness, hostility, anger.
       Note - because anger is wrongly considered by many Christians to be unacceptable, we often say we are hurt when we really mean angry, or resentful.
    c. Jealousy, envy.
    d. Guilt, regret, remorse, condemnation.
    e. Fear, dread, anxiety.
    f. Indifference, apathy (death of a relationship).

3. **The result in our behaviour may be either**
    a. Aggression, conflict, strife, contention, confrontation (fight).
    b. Withdrawal, avoidance (flight).

Restoring Broken Relationships

The distortion or breakdown of relationships is one of the painful results of the Fall. (Genesis 3:16, 4:1-15).

The possibility of reconciliation is grounded in the work of the cross. (See Chapter 3). It is the basis not only for reconciling man to God, but also for reconciling man to man (Ephesians 2:11; Galatians 3:27-8). This means that:

1. **We cannot reconcile people by trying to deal with the accumulated problems.** This places a weight on an already fragile relationship that it usually cannot bear.
2. **Only persons can be reconciled.** The relationship needs a new base on which to stand, to be able to tackle the problems. Only when the parties are reconciled as persons, can the behavioural and attitudinal problems be successfully faced.
3. **We have to make a clear distinction between the person and his or her behaviour.** In a troubled

relationship the parties have usually lost each other in the welter of problems.

The Model for Reconciliation

1. When we come to Christ for salvation we are conscious of our alienated state, rather than the memory or catalogue of our sins and failures.

    We may recall some of our sins as representative or illustrative of our state, but God does not restore us on the basis of our dealing with our problems.

    Out of his grace, and by virtue of Christ's death on the Cross, we are received by God and restored into a new relationship.

Salvation is therefore the model for restoring relationships at any level.

2. Our ongoing relationship with God, called sanctification, does not involve the solving of the problems between us and God. It is based on:
    a. **An assurance of our secure acceptance** by God on the basis of the work of Christ on the Cross. This acceptance does not depend, then or ever, on our success in problem solving.
    b. The Holy Spirit leads us into **progressive specific repentance** for sins and sinful attitudes.
    c. We face up to **progressive changes in character and lifestyle** to harmonise more and more with the character and nature of God. (Romans 8:29; 2 Corinthians 3:18).
    d. There is **an increasing fulfilment and joy as we learn to live for God's glory and pleasure, not our own.**

Sanctification is therefore the model for problem-solving in relationships. When we are secure in our acceptance by each other, we have the courage to face up to the task of correcting wrong behaviour and making the

141

necessary changes in our acts and attitudes. We experience joy and fulfilment as we learn to live for one another and not for ourselves.

Preparation for reconciliation

The parties need to prepare themselves for reconciliation. We need to remember that:
1. **In a broken relationship there is never all the fault on one side and none on the other.** We have both, therefore been guilty of wrong actions and/or wrong reactions (1 Corinthians 1:11, 3:4; Galatians 5:19-20).
2. **Our capacity for self justification and self deception is enormous.** We need the Holy Spirit to search our hearts and reveal the truth (Matthew 7:1-5; Psalm 139:23-24). We should, therefore, act in a spirit of humble gentleness toward the other person, being aware of our own weaknesses and failings. (Galatians 6:1-2).
3. **We are always the ones who have to take the initiative.**
   a. If our brother has something against us - we are to go to him (Matthew 5:23f).
   b. If we have something against our brother - we are to go to him (Matthew 18:15f).
   c. If our brother hates us he is in darkness; if we do not hate him we are in the light. If he is in the dark he cannot find us. If we are in the light we can find him (1 John 2:10-11).
4. **Reconciliation only works on the basis of grace.**
   a. Grace is God's initiative. Grace therefore requires that we also take the initiative. (see 3 above.)
   b. Grace is doing good with no strings attached. It is being willing to go all the way unconditionally.
   To say - "I will do this if you do that", is not grace but works.
   To say - "I've come half way therefore you must come the other half", is not grace but law.
5. **We must deal unilaterally with the question of resentment and bitterness.** (Ephesians 4:31).

a. Because we have been forgiven we must be willing to forgive (Ephesians 4:32; Matthew 18:23f).
b. Forgiveness is letting go of what we have been holding against the other person. It is a decision of our will.
c. If we hold on to bitterness
    i. We shut Christ out. He cannot heal the hurt, if by so doing he appears to justify our bitter feelings.
    ii. We remain under the power of the situation. We are not free to choose how we will feel or behave towards the other person.

The process of reconciliation

In restoring a broken relationship, the accumulation of problems have to temporarily be put on one side so that the person can be reconciled. There then has to be a mutual acknowledgement of failure and alienation from one another.

1. We acknowledge we have sinned against and grieved the Holy Spirit by the breach in our relationship.
2. We acknowledge that we have sinned by acting or reacting unlovingly against each other.
3. In some cases we may have broken vows that we made to each other, for example in the marriage covenant. Therefore we have been guilty of covenant breaking.
4. We repent of these sins and ask and receive God's forgiveness.
5. We ask forgiveness from and give forgiveness to each other.
6. We accept by faith a new beginning in Christ, in which we also acknowledge that there are ways in which we will need to change.
7. We accept or receive each other just as Christ has received us, that is,
    a. As persons.
    b. Into a new relationship.
    c. On the basis of grace.

8. We undertake to build a new relationship on the ongoing basis of mutual love, trust, respect and understanding.

Dealing with relationship problems

In the ongoing adjustment of the new relationship we may have to face up to many problems. They will fall into a number of different classes.

1. **Things that call for forbearance not action**
    Forebearance is not being unduly disturbed or chafed by the faults and ignorance of others. (Ephesians 4:2; Hebrews 5:1-2, 12:3; Mark 9:19).
    a. It has to do with things in the other person that rub us or irritate us.
    b. It is not mere tolerance but the deliberate bearing of one another's weaknesses. (Romans 15:1-2).
    c. It is a priestly ministry, therefore its source is Christ our High Priest. (Hebrews 2:17f, 4:15f)
2. **Anger or wrong reaction due not primarily to the other person's behaviour** but to:
    a. Unresolved hurts or difficulties in our own past that have nothing to do with the other person, for example childhood hurts or fears.
    b. Areas of hardness in our hearts that God wants to deal with.
    c. Unyielded rights that God wants us to surrender to Him. When our rights are ignored or infringed we can get angry. The solution is the yielding of those rights to the Lordship of Christ.
3. **Grievances or offences that have to be faced and dealt with.**
    These may be due to:
    a. **Misunderstanding or mistake.** The answer is to clear up the misunderstanding. Always choose to believe in the other person's good intentions and to credit him with the best motives, not the worst. (1 Corinthians 13:7). Remember that if a person makes a mistake, even a stupid one, he is not lying

unless he knows the truth and deliberately twists it.

b. **Unintentional wrongs.** The other person may have wronged me but not intended it, or he may not even be aware that he has wronged me. If there was no intention to hurt, I cannot hold it against the other person. I am not even entitled to forgive him, and to express forgiveness may leave him feeling he has been unjustly judged. If I have unintentionally hurt the other person, I should express sorrow or regret and learn from my mistakes. Stupidity or insensitivity may become blameworthy if I do not correct it.

c. **Wrongs which have occurred**

    i. If you have wronged another person do not apologise - an apology often avoids an admission that we have committed an offence. Acknowledge the wrong and ask forgiveness. Restitution may sometimes be necessary.

    ii. If you have been wronged, note the proper function of anger. (Ephesians 4:26; Mark 3:1-5). Anger is an arousal emotion to move us to act, to correct an injustice, or to protect ourselves or those we love against threat or harm; to seek an apology, restitution or retribution for a wrong; to protect ourselves or other people from a repetition of the offence; to let the other person know how we feel so that he has a chance to change his behaviour.

    iii. If the other person responds with repentance then we must forgive (Luke 17:3-4).

    iv. If redress or correction cannot be achieved, then we must unilaterally forgive. This avoids the continuance of resentment (to feel over and over again).

    v. Note the danger of premature forgiveness that breeds resentment.

    vi. Once something has been repented of and forgiven, it must never be brought up again. Forgiveness says in effect:

I will never mention this to you again
I will never mention it to anyone else again
I will never mention it to myself again (in self pity or self indulgence).

4. **Where attitudes or behaviour patterns need to be changed,** the process is:

   a. Identify the wrong behaviour and stop it (Put off the old. Ephesians 4:22).

   b. Change our perceptions as to what is appropriate. (Be renewed in your mind. Ephesians 4:23).

   c. Learn new and more appropriate behaviour. (Put on the new. Ephesians 4:24)

5. **Separate relational problems from personal problems.**

   a. Relational problems are those that concern the relationship between the parties.

   b. Personal problems are the problems a person has in his or her private life, distinct from and quite apart from the relationship.

The extent to which these personal problems can be touched without invitation is very limited, even in relationships of great intimacy and scope, unless the other person has clearly given us that right. Relationships are often unnecessarily confused and disturbed, because one party or the other seeks to intrude into the other's privacy to help them with a problem.

Scriptures on Relationships - the "one another" syndrome

Love

1. **Love** one another (John 13:34; 15:12,17; Romans 12:10, 13:8; 1 Thessalonians 4:9; 1 Peter 1:22, 4:8; 1 John 3:11, 4:7).

2. **Care** for one another (1 Corinthians 12:25).

3. **Accept** one another (Romans 15:7).

4. **Be kind** to one another (Ephesians 4:32).

5. **Be tender-hearted** to one another (Ephesians 4:32).

6. **Comfort one another** (1 Thessalonians 4:18).

7. **Serve one another** (1 Peter 4:10).
8. **Bear one another's burdens** (Galatians 6:2).
9. **Greet one another with a kiss** (1 Corinthians 16:20; 2 Corinthians 13:12; 1 Peter 5:14).
10. **Be hospitable to one another** (1 Peter 4:9).
11. **Pray for one another** (James 5:16).
12. **Stimulate** one another to love and good deeds (Hebrews 10:24).
13. **Show forbearance** to one another (Ephesians 4:2).
14. **Forgive** one another (Ephesians 4:32; Colossians 3:13).
15. **Stop depriving** one another (1 Corinthians 7:5). You shall not wrong one another (Leviticus 25:14).
16. **Seek after that which is good** for one another (1 Thessalonians 5:15).
17. **Wash** one another's feet (John 13:14).

Trust
18. **Be subject** to one another (Ephesians 5:21).
19. **Confess your** sins to one another (James 5:16).
20. **Be of the same mind** with one another (Romans 12:16, 15:5).
21. **Do not lie** to one another (Colossians 3:9). Speak the truth to one another (Zechariah 8:16).
22. **Do not speak against** one another (James 5:9).
23. **Do not complain against** one another (James 5:9).
24. **Do not have law suits against** one another (1 Corinthians 6:7), not challenging one another, envying one another (Galatians 5:26).

Respect
25. **Encourage** one another (1 Thessalonians 5:11; Hebrews 3:13).
26. **Build one another** up (Romans 14:9; 1 Thessalonians 5:11).
27. **Members** of another (Romans 12:5).
28. **Give preference** to one another in honour (Romans 12:10).
29. **Regard one** another as more important than yourself (Philippians 2:3).
30. **Clothe yourselves with humility** towards one another (1 Peter 5:5).

Understanding

31. **Have fellowship** with one another (1 John 1:7).
32. **Be at peace** with one another (Mark 9:50; Romans 14:19).
33. **Teach** one another (Colossians 3:16).
34. **Admonish** one another (Romans 15:14; Colossians 3:16).
35. **Speaking** to one another (Ephesians 5:19).

Summary

A relationship is the mutual sharing of life between two or more parties. They can be instrumental, that is a means to an end, or they can be consummatory, that is an end in themselves. Relationships are also of varying degrees of intimacy and occupy varying amounts of the lives of the participants. Intimacy and scope do not necessarily go together, a relationship may be limited in extent or time and yet involve very great intimacy during its existence.

There are four factors that are involved in building healthy relationships - love or care, trust, respect or honour and understanding or knowledge. Each has to be given adequate attention. If any of them is neglected or adversely affected, the relationship comes under stress; if the failure is not addressed or rectified the relationship begins to break down. The resulting trauma has effects on the parties' mental, emotional and behavioural states, generally in direct importance to the intimacy or the scope of the relationship. The distortion or breakdown of relationships is one of the results of the Fall. Reconciliation is one of the results of the Cross. Christ not only made possible the reconciliation of man and God but the reconciliation of man and man. Salvation thus becomes the model for all forms of reconciliation, from which we understand that problem solving is not the method to be used. Only persons can be reconciled. When we are reconciled to God, problem solving is what God does not do - He restores us into a relationship with Himself by grace on the basis of the work of the cross. Persons must be restored on the same basis. Problem solving is possible only after reconciliation, so sanctification becomes the model for problem solving in relationships - we can face the problems because we now have a secure base on which to stand, and our acceptance of each other no longer depends on our success in solving the problems.

In dealing with the problems that arise in relationships, note the important place of forbearance. Most difficulties only become problems because the persons are already becoming distant from each other. When serious problems do arise they need to be faced openly, honestly, frankly and if fault is present it needs to be freely confessed and as freely forgiven so that the difficulties and adjustments become growing points.

11
What Happens After Healing?

Divine healing is not a mere temporary improvement or a remission of symptoms. It is a complete cure, a restoration of the body or soul to the wholeness or health that is meant by God to be its normal state.

God never takes back what he has given. No true father would demand back what he had freely given to his children (Romans 11:29; Matthew 15:26). Healing, if it is "lost", is forfeited either because we are at fault, or because we have allowed Satan to rob us of it. He will use various means, for example, discouragement, negative influences or deceptive symptoms. This is particularly the case when healing is not instantaneous, but takes place over a period.

Two aspects need to be considered; the first is how to establish the healing so that it is permanent, the second is how to seek to live in divine health.

We will look first at the steps we need to take to establish healing, particularly in the early stages.

Establishing the Healing

Everything that God does for us requires our human co-operation or response. This is a mark of God's regard for us as persons. We are never machines to be tinkered with, but persons to be saved, or healed, or set free. This is why a faith response is always required, both to receive from God, and also to retain what He has given us. *"It is for freedom that Christ has set us free. Stand firm, then, and do not let yourselves be burdened again by a yoke of slavery"* (Galatians 5:1).

In establishing healing or deliverance, two factors are of particular importance.

1. Obedience. The first appearance of a truth in Scripture is always important, because it lays down the normative conditions that generally govern all future interpretations. In terms of healing, Exodus 15:26 is crucial, because it establishes obedience to God as a basic principle of health and healing. *"If you listen carefully to the voice of the Lord your God and do what is right in his eyes, if you pay attention to his commands and keep all his decrees, I will not bring on you any of the diseases I brought on the Egyptians, for I am the Lord who heals you"*.

    If we put ourselves under a doctor's care, we put ourselves under his authority and direction. If we ignore his instructions and prescriptions, and insist on going our own way, the likelihood is that he would walk off the case. Similarly, when we are in the hands of the Good Physician, we must accept his direction for our whole life and life-style. Obedience is more than ever necessary in the experience of healing, because God may well be reordering things in our life that brought the sickness or hurt in the first place.

2. Confession. The instrument God uses to heal us is his word, because his words and his works are one and the same thing.

    "The words I say to you are not just my own. Rather, it is the Father, living in me, who is doing his works" (John 14:10).

    It is the word of God that is spirit and life (John 6:63), that creates faith (Romans 10:17), and that heals (Psalm 107:20). It was when the word of Jesus was believed that miracles happened (John 4:50).

    Confession is agreeing with what God says. It is speaking his word into existence by our lips, and also by our actions and our attitudes of heart.

    We have already dealt with the vital link between faith and confession in the appropriation of the promises of God. God's promises are a real provision for our needs, but this provision remains only potential, until faith reaches out and receives it. Even so, the provision may be received, but still remain only latent until confession actualises it in experience. Suppose, for example, I am about to go to prison for not paying a debt. A friend says, "I have enough money to meet your debt. It is yours, if you want it". I now have access to provision, but I could still go to gaol if I do nothing about it. I ask him for the money and he pays it into my bank account. I now have the provision, but I could still be gaoled as a debtor, unless I draw a cheque and hand it over in payment of my debts. Confession is that kind of drawing on what we have already received in our faith. *"If you confess with your mouth ... and believe in your heart ... you will be saved* (made whole)" (Romans 10:9).

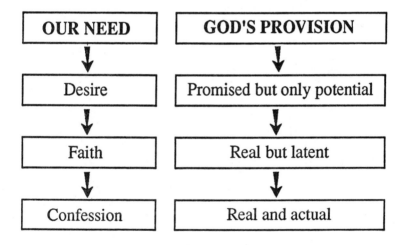

OUR NEED	GOD'S PROVISION
Desire	Promised but only potential
Faith	Real but latent
Confession	Real and actual

We overcome Satan by the Blood of the Lamb and word of our testimony (Revelation 12:11). Here is one way in which we can use the word of God, and the confession of that word, in order to confirm and establish healing.

1. Get from God a word of healing for your particular

situation. This may be one of the general healing promises of scripture, or it may be a passage that has a particular application to your personal situation, or one that the Holy Spirit specifically draws to your attention. Meditate and pray over the scripture so that the Holy Spirit can quicken it to you and it becomes revelation truth.

2. Confess the scripture aloud. Do it several times a day. Confession will speak the word into your own heart where it will create faith. Speak it against Satan. *"It is written ..."* (Matthew 4:4). Thus the word of God becomes a shield between you and the doubts and fears the devil would plant in your heart (Ephesians 6:16). Speak it to God, declaring your confidence in his word *"fully persuaded that God had power to do what he had promised"* (Romans 4:21).

3. Persist in your confession (Hebrews 4:14). It is a work or a fight of faith. Remember that the word (rhema) of God is spirit and life. Words are the vehicle of spirit (Ephesians 6:17) therefore the words carry the very truth they express. When I confess "By his wounds you have been healed" the healing is in the words themselves (1 Peter 2:24).

How Healing may be Lost

Not only do the healing miracles of Jesus show the keys for healing in different situations, they also include important information regarding ways in which it can be lost. In particular, we can lose healing or deliverance by:

1. Continuing in known sin. To the paralytic he had healed at the pool Bethesda Jesus said *"See, you are well again. Stop sinning or something worse may happen to you"* (John 5:14).

    God will always be true to his nature in dealing with sin. We cannot presume upon his grace or assume that, because he has healed us, he will overlook sin that we are not willing to be done with.

2. Exposure to unbelief and negativity. It seems clear that

corporate unbelief was such a hindrance to healing, that on occasions Jesus took steps to separate the needy person from the surrounding unbelief (Mark 5:40). In healing the blind man from Bethsaida (Mark 8:23-26), Jesus took him right outside the village and, after he was healed, sent him home saying, *"Don't go into the village"*. Bethsaida was a town whose unbelief was notorious, in spite of the miracles it had seen (Matthew 11:21).

We can lose our healing, or fail to have a potential healing established, by exposure to the corrosive effect of unbelief and negative thought.

3. Premature testimony. There seems to be significance in the occasions when Jesus forbade the healed person to testify (Matthew 9:30; Mark 7:31-36). With the leper in Matthew 8:4, Jesus sent him first to obtain a clearance from the priest.

There are occasions when too early a claim of healing puts more pressure on the person's faith than it is able to stand at the time. Jesus seems to have been aware of this contingency, which is why he was often at pains to explain to the person the basis of their healing (Mark 5:30-34).

4. Deceptive symptoms. Satan will always seek to rob us of what God has given. The area of our sickness, fear, or hurt, remains for a period an area of vulnerability that Satan will attack. Unless we stand firm on what God has done, we can be deceived into thinking we have lost it. This is particularly the case with inner healing. Peter, for example, had a problem with fear of man that led him to deny Christ. In John Chapter 21 we have the record of Jesus dealing with this need in Peter's life, so that on the day of Pentecost Peter is totally free. Yet years later in Antioch the same fear of man led Peter to separate himself from the Gentile believers (Galatians 2:11-12).

In the area of recurring symptoms, the power of confession is all important. In other words, we do not keep going back to our body (or mind or feelings) to see if we are healed; we go to the word to see if we are healed.

5. Neglecting God-given laws of health, for example rest, diet and care for the body (Ephesians 5:29; Colossians 2:23; Mark 2:27; 1 Corinthians 3:16). Because our body is a temple of the Holy Spirit, we are to care for it, and respect its needs. See later in "Living in Divine Health".

How Healing is Retained

Avoiding or overcoming the things that work against healing, helps us to retain it; but there are other positive factors that are also important. Note the following:

1. Don't make provision to stay sick. In several instances we find that Jesus made sure that the healed person immediately began to function in health instead of sickness. '"*Get up, take your mat and go home*" (Mark 2:11; John 5:8).

    For healing to be retained I may need to readjust my mental attitude from, "I am a sick person" to, "I am a well person"; or from, "I am inadequate and afraid and rejected", to "I am accepted in the Beloved. I can do all things through Christ."

2. Understand the basis for your healing. If we are healed, but do not really understand how or why, we may lose it because we do not know how to hold on to it. We must, therefore, set ourselves to understand the way God works and the grounds of his dealings with us. For this reason, Jesus did not leave the woman, who was healed by touching the hem of his garment, in ignorance. He explained the faith basis of her cure (Luke 8:47-48. See also Matthew 15:28 and Mark 10:52).

3. Be thankful. Of the ten lepers who were healed, only one, a Samaritan, returned to give glory to God (Luke 17:11-19). Paul specifies ingratitude as a root of man's sin (Romans 1:21). It is failing to give honour and glory to God as the source of life and health. Few sins are so

156

characteristic of selfishness (2 Timothy 3:2), and few things are more damaging to health than self-centredness.

4. See the healing as a means to go on to know Christ better. The nobleman (whose son was healed) went on from believing the word of Jesus, to believing in Jesus (John 4:50,53). The man born blind grew in his understanding from *"the man called Jesus"* (John 9:11), to *"a prophet"* (v 17), to *"the Son of Man"* and *"Lord"* (v 35-38). When healing becomes an end in itself, we can lose it. When it becomes an experience of growing relationship with the Healer, we will never lose it.

5. Sometimes we may need to get medical confirmation of our healing. This is not doubt (Mark 1:44), but a testimony for the glory of God, and should always be done when it means giving up medicines or ceasing treatment.

6. Testify to those nearest to you. Repeatedly, those that Jesus healed and delivered were sent to their homes to testify. *"Return home and tell how much God has done for you"* (Luke 8:39). It is in our homes that the reality of what God has done can be most clearly seen, and will carry the greatest impact.

7. Nourish the restored health. When Jairus' daughter is raised up by the power of God, Jesus orders a meal for her. The widow of Nain's son is handed over for some mothering (Luke 7:11-17, 8:40-56). Sometimes when the Lord brings to life a long dead or destroyed part of the personality, it is like being a temporary father or mother to part of what is still a child.

8. Get rid of the graveclothes (John 11:44). This is similar to No 7 but may go further. We have to get rid of all the sick attitudes, inhibitions, dependencies and so on that hamper and restrict the new life that has come to us in healing.

9. Use your restored health to enable you to serve others (Mark 1:31). Sickness, especially if it is prolonged, has a tendency to make us self-centred and accustomed to being ministered to. Correct that imbalance by being ready to serve others.

10. Where there has been deliverance from demonic domination, fill the vacancy (Luke 11:14-28).
11. If we have not already done so, be obedient to the Lord in baptism, both in water and the Holy Spirit (Acts 9:17-19). The old life with its failings and its weaknesses is buried, and we enter into the power of life (Romans 6:4, 8:11).

Living in Divine Health

The aim of all healing is restoration to health. God's will for us is not only healing, but health, the state summed up in the Hebrew as "shalom", well-being. *"Dear friend, I pray that you may enjoy good health and that all may go well with you, even as your soul is getting along well"* (3 John 2).

What is in view is the wholeness of life. Physical and mental well-being are closely associated; it is equally clear that spiritual health is bound up with health of mind and body.

There is a great deal still to be learned about the biblical principles of divine health for believers, but the following points are suggested for further thought.

1. Human nature, at all levels, was created to function in harmony with the law of God. Therefore when the commandments are built into our life as active righteousness, they will produce health (Proverbs 3:2, 7-8, 4:21-22).

   The life of the believer is thus to be characterised by moderation, gratitude and sanctified common sense (1 Timothy 2:3-5, 7-8, 6:6).

2. Salvation in the Bible is not only in terms of past guilt and alienation (Ephesians 2:8), but is also a "being saved" now from its power and effect on our lives (1 Corinthians 1:18). Ultimately it will be salvation from the very presence of sin and from every vestige of its effect (Romans 5:10; 8:18-25; 1 Peter 1:9).

   The freedom of the sons of God includes freedom from corruption, of which we have received the first fruits of the Spirit (Romans 8:21,23).

3. Jesus came that we might have life more abundantly (John 10:10). This life, the life of Jesus, is intended to be manifested in our mortal bodies (2 Corinthians 4:10-11).

   The Holy Spirit who is the Spirit of life, indwells the believer's body and gives it that life. *"He who raised Christ from the dead will also give life to your mortal bodies through his Spirit, who lives in you"* (Romans 8:11).

4. It is clear from Scripture, that the believer who walks in the love and fear of the Lord is meant to expect good health well into old age, and strength appropriate to his years. *"With long life will I satisfy him and show him my salvation"* (Psalm 91:16). *"You will come to the grave in full vigour, like sheaves gathered in season"* (Job 5:26). We must expect all the normal signs of ageing, but not necessarily extreme weakness or senility, nor a painful and lingering illness at the end (Deuteronomy 33:25). Rather there should be a speedy ebbing away of life, as the Lord takes the believer to himself, or a peaceful yielding up of his life at the end, to be *"with Christ which is far better."*

Summary

The vulnerable period is immediately after the healing or deliverance, when we may have difficulty in resisting the temptation to give way to old fears, symptoms, and doubts.

Two factors are vital. The first is obedience to the Lord, not just over the healing, but over every area of our life. Healing and obedience are always linked. The second is the daily confession of the word to God, to Satan and ourselves. Since there is life and healing in the word, confession will deal with the symptoms. Without confession, God's provision - real though it is - may remain only latent within us.

Healing may be "lost" through continuance in known sin, through exposure to unbelief and negative influences, through premature testimony, by satanically produced symptoms or by our neglect of the God-given laws of health.

For healing to be retained, the keys include an inner orientation towards health rather than sickness; an understanding of the basis of our healing so that we can hold on to it, and gratitude as a state of heart. We must see healing as a means to trust and love the Healer more, and give testimony, particularly to those at home. In some cases medical confirmation of healing should be sought. We also need to nourish the restored life, get rid of wrong attitudes or habits, and yield recovered areas of our life to the Holy Spirit.

Also by Tom Marshall

Free Indeed, how to live free in spirit, soul and body.

Right Relationships, a biblical foundation
for making and mending relationships.

Understanding Leadership